MOMENTUM

13 Lessons from Action Takers

Who Changed the World

by

Lynda Sunshine West

Foreword by

Don Green

Executive Director, The Napoleon Hill Foundation

Women Action Takers™ Publishing
San Diego, California

Women Action Takers™ Publishing
www.womenactiontakers.com

ebook ISBN: 978-1-7348759-1-1
Paperback ISBN: 978-1-7348759-0-4

Editorial services by GMK Writing and Editing, Inc.
Cover Design by D V Suresh
Printed in the United States of America

Table of Contents

Foreword by Don Green, Executive Director, The Napoleon

    Hill Foundation   5

A Sunny Note from Lynda   7

Part One: The Challenging Climb

Wise Man #1: Ron Klein   11

Chapter One: Combatting the Negative - *Annie Evans*   13

Chapter Two: Living Life on Purpose - *David Blackford*   21

Chapter Three: Imagining the Dream - *Nadia Fleury*   31

Chapter Four: Taking Little Steps - *Krysten Maracle*   41

Part Two: Touching Down on the Top

Wise Man #2: Dr. Greg Reid   49

Chapter Five: Connecting with "the Cashflow Chick" -

    Paige Panzarello   51

Chapter Six: Following the *Ask Method - Amy Burton*   59

Chapter Seven: Acting *As If...*When Achieving a Goal -

    Annie Evans   73

Part Three: Maximum Momentum

Wise Man #3: Frank Shankwitz   83

Chapter Eight: Being Authentic - *Sohaila Handelsman*   85

Chapter Nine: Winning People Over with Charisma –

    Michael (Mike) Packman   95

Chapter Ten: Cooperating and Collaborating—Not Competing -

    Dennis Haber   105

Part Four: Final Finish

Wise Man #4: Brian Smith   117

Chapter Eleven: Deciding to Be Determined, Driven—and

    Focused - *Elizabeth Moors*   121

Chapter Twelve: Leading Others with Courage to Fearless

    Freedom - *Kym Glass*   135

Bonus: Keeping the Momentum Going—Cutting Yourself (and

    Others) Some Slack – *Pati Maez*   147

Contributor Biographies   161

Be brave and share your weaknesses, for in your weaknesses, others see your strengths.

—Lynda Sunshine West

MOMENTUM

Foreword

by Don Green, Executive Director,
The Napoleon Hill Foundation

Education is simply a bridge that takes you from where you are to where you want to go. Most people learn in one of two ways—by reading books or by being associated with people who are smarter than they are. I have found that reading books is a great way to learn, and I believe you will gain a tremendous amount of knowledge by this excellent book by Lynda Sunshine West.

Lynda has done a superb job compiling the thoughts of a dozen contributors who will help you by relating their own experiences and what worked for them. These special individuals are entrepreneurs, small business owners, speakers, trainers, and professionals in a range of areas who have "been there, done that" and have a wonderful passion for wanting to help others on their journeys. You will be informed, entertained, and inspired by them, as well as the four remarkable "Wise Men" Lynda encounters along the way.

After you have read *Momentum*, be sure to apply what you have learned to your own life. It is often said that knowledge is power. However, I believe it is only *potential* power and must be backed by *action*, if you want to see results. As Napoleon Hill wrote, "Create a definite plan for carrying out your desire and begin at once, whether you are ready or not, to put this plan into action."

As a former bank president for about twenty years, I am often asked about financial issues and investments. I believe that the best investment you will ever make is not in a stock or bond, but the one you make in yourself. By reading this book, you will be making an excellent investment in yourself.

5

MOMENTUM

A Sunny Note from Lynda

Welcome to *Momentum*!

If you've picked up this book, chances are you are an entrepreneur who is stuck while facing a daunting challenge. Or maybe you are someone who just needs a pep talk to help get you through a difficult time.

We all need a boost every now and then to help us climb our personal mountains. There is no shame whatsoever in asking for help from an expert. The only shame, perhaps, is not receiving such a gift with gratitude when it is placed before us—whether we are able to follow the advice or not.

I've been blessed by having had so many people assist me on my journey, and I want you to know that you are not alone while you are on yours. I have your back—as do all of the wonderful contributors to this book. Know that there is a solution to every problem and someone knowledgeable in your circle of contacts is ready, willing, and able to help you. All you need to do is *ask*! (For more on that subject, see Chapter Six…)

If you do happen to stumble backwards—as I have on numerous occasions—you must get right back up on your feet and learn from your experience. You will be amazed at how failure often leads to even greater opportunity and success down the road.

Why *Momentum*?

You can't succeed in any business venture without having *momentum*.

In science, *momentum* is "mass in motion." In my mind, *gaining momentum* in business means you have created the right environment to enable one success to build upon another. When this occurs, your business experiences greater force, intensity, and speed, which means one thing: *growth*!

My goal—which is shared among all of the contributors to this book—is to add all of our collective momentum to yours. We want to see you accomplish all of your dreams and goals and flourish.

What Is This Book About?

Although *Momentum* may seem like a memoir at times, it is far from that genre. This is not "Lynda's story." In fact, the main intent of this book is to spotlight the content of the contributors in a way that is accessible, actionable, and, hopefully, entertaining.

I would characterize this book as a business (non-religious) success parable—a simple story that is intended to provide brief lessons that are intended to help you address and problem-solve issues related to your business. (For further reference, I encourage you to read classic parables, such *as Three Feet from Gold*, by Sharon Lechter and Dr. Greg Reid; *The Five Dysfunctions of a Team*, by Patrick Lencioni; and *The Go-Giver*, by Bob Burg and John David Mann.) My journey of climbing a metaphorical mountain is based on fact, but some creative license has obviously been taken in order to breathe life to the situations that unfold in the chapters.

The backgrounds and accomplishments of the contributors are all true. Their observations, principles, and lessons are 100% authentic to their business practices and philosophies. All of these brilliant individuals—as well as the four wise people who introduce each part section—were an integral part of developing the content for this book. *Momentum* would not have been possible without them. Please feel free to contact them via their web sites—they would love to hear from you!

I humbly dedicate this book to all of these wonderful folks, who have served as an inspiration to me:

David Blackford, Amy Burton, Annie Evans, Nadia Fleury, Kym Glass, Don Green, Dennis Haber, Sohaila Handelsman, Ron Klein, Pati Maez, Krysten Maracle, Elizabeth Moors, Mike Packman, Paige Panzarello, Dr. Greg S. Reid, Frank Shankwitz, and Brian Smith

A Special Note About the Charity

The proceeds from this work are being donated to The Giving Angels—a 501(c)(3) nonprofit whose mission is to eradicate homelessness once and for all. To learn more about The Giving Angels, please visit **www.TheGivingAngels.org**.

MOMENTUM

Part One

Wise Man #1

Ron Klein

Momentum.

Where does one start?

In order to begin your journey, you must first identify the challenge. By this I mean identifying a need or want and providing the solution. Once you have done that, you must rid yourself of any fears—especially of failure—and tackle the challenge right away.

In my mind, there is no such thing as failure. If you make a mistake, all you need to do is learn from it, be daring, and change direction. Let's say you paint a collage in the wrong color the first time. So what? You repaint it a different color. Move on.

I look at every challenge as a little house with a front door. Before I even take a step in that house, I make sure there's a back door in case I need to get out and start over in another house.

In order to remain focused on the challenge and see it through, you must have three things: a *mission*, a *vision*, and a *purpose*. I have my own interpretations of all three of these concepts.

A *mission* is what you do, how you enhance it, how you function, how you intend to run your business, and how you plan to collaborate with other people. Your *mission* is *you*. It's the value that you bring to whatever you are working on.

Your *vision* is your ultimate roadmap to be the best at

whatever you are doing in order to fulfill your *mission*. You want to *think big* with your *vision* and soar.

The last thing, *purpose*, is perhaps the most difficult. *Purpose* is your *why*. It's like a compass as a constant reminder of where you are and urging you forward to keep pursuing your *vision* and *mission*. Your *purpose* provides you with the motivation you need to sustain your commitment from beginning to end, no matter what challenges and obstacles might come your way.

Next comes the actual execution and steps needed to start your business or create a product. You can't go wrong if you are trying to help people solve a problem.

Sometimes this means solving a problem people didn't know even existed. You are just making something faster and easier for people. This often happens through product improvements or enhancements. I accomplished this through numerous inventions, including the magnetic strip on credit cards.

I believe virtually anything can be made different and better—even something as simple as a paper clip!

The following contributors will be standing right by your side as you make your challenging climb up the mountain: *Annie Evans*, *David (Dave) Blackford*, *Nadia Fleury*, and *Krysten Maracle*.

Chapter One

Combatting the Negative

Annie Evans

They say you never know who you might be standing next to. It could end up being the one individual who will change your life. Annie Evans unknowingly became one such person to me.

Several years ago, I found myself on a long line at a drugstore awaiting my prescription. It felt like it was taking an eternity, which always seems to be the case when you're stressed out and have too much on your plate. Not only was just one person working the register, she was without a doubt the slowest cashier in history. Naturally, a half dozen people were ahead of me: the first fumbled in her wallet to find the right credit card; the second had a billion questions about her prescriptions; the third insisted on handing his ten dollar copayment one coin at a time in quarters, dimes, nickels, and pennies; the fourth tried to get away with using an expired coupon from the 1970s and argued with the cashier when she rejected it; and the two people ahead of me lugged overloaded baskets full of goods toward the counter.

During my wait, I had plenty of time to ruminate about my looming career journey. It felt like I was staring up at an insurmountable mountain. I was scared to death.

I'll never succeed starting my video training business. I've already lost 70K on one business venture. I'm doomed to fail again. How can I scale this mountain when I'm too scared to even begin?

The customer paying with change spilled several coins on the floor and groaned as he bent down to pick them up one at a time.

My eyes rolled back inside my head.

My neck craned back in frustration.

My foot stomped in place.

"I'm never getting out of here," I grumbled, clenching my fists.

"Feeling a bit tense?," asked a female voice behind me.

I became irritated that a total stranger had the audacity to interrupt my brooding. I turned around sharply. At first, I was prepared to lash out with something along the lines of "Mind your own business" but, when I caught sight of the woman's face, the words wouldn't come out of my lips. There was something about her wide smile that seemed warm and inviting. Her funky-shaped eyeglass frames made her seem sophisticated and smart.

"Don't worry, I'm not needling you," she said, revealing her perfect set of teeth through her continuing smile. "I'm just as frustrated as you are with this line."

"You don't *seem* all that frustrated."

"Oh, I am," she admitted, adjusting her glasses. "I just choose to see it differently, so it feels different."

"Really? How do you manage that?"

"It's a difficult concept," she explained. "You see, I believe that the subconscious controls our lives. Our minds tell us things and we just accept them. You see a long line and automatically assume it's a waste of time. I see a long line, too. But instead of dwelling on it I choose to think about something positive—like the interesting person standing right in front of me. I notice she's struggling with something and wonder what it is. I know it's not about this long wait."

14

"Is it that obvious?," I glared.

"Frankly, yes—but whatever it is, maybe I can help," she answered, extending her hand. "My name is Annie."

"I'm Lynda," I said, shaking her hand.

"Nice to meet you, Lynda. Tell me: What is troubling you?"

I admit I felt a bit intimidated by her and uncomfortable over-sharing with a stranger, but something compelled me to dive right in and spill everything. I guess it was all boiling up inside and I needed to vent to someone. "A few years ago, I quit my crusty job working for a judge in the court of appeals. Since then, I've been floundering trying to make money creating one business after another. Now I have another new one—a video training and coaching company for women—and I'm starting to have doubts all over again. I've put my husband and me—*everything*—in jeopardy."

She paused, soaking in what I'd just said: something clicked. Her body language tilted toward me, as if she were a sister confiding in me about a big secret. "As it happens, Lynda, I'm an expert at starting over. I've had to start over many times, and I needed to learn how to heal myself of anger, grief, and other periods of great upset that I've been through in my life."

She swallowed and took a deep breath in preparation for what she was about to share. "My mother was a beautiful debutante from a split-up but fairly wealthy family. She suffered from mental illness, but no one acknowledged it until at least ten years after I was born. One of my earliest memories is her telling me that I was a monster because she believed I bit her after I was born from a C-section. That sounds hard to believe because most babies are born without teeth, but she was convinced of this and repeated it to me throughout my life. She was volatile and really hard on me—physically at times, but mostly emotionally abusive. Eventually, she was arrested and institutionalized. She spent a lot of time in mental hospitals over the course of her life. I grew up pretty angry and negative, spending a lot of time battling my demons."

I placed my arm on her shoulder. I hesitated at first, not knowing what to say. My challenges paled in comparison with hers. "I'm so sorry..."

"That's hardly the end of it," she continued. "My brother was also diagnosed with mental illness when he was in his 30s and 40s. Not only that, but my ex-life partner, his new girlfriend, and other crew members were lost at sea in a storm, along with the boat. I didn't go on this trip, but I'd left my prized possessions aboard—so I lost everything."

"My goodness!"

"I've had more than my share of challenges and tragedy, but I've lived my life on my own terms. I've chosen love and adventure over money many times. I've also started over many times. I've done everything from training horses and fashion design to product development and international supply chain management...then I flipped from the corporate workplace to be an entrepreneur."

"You're an *entrepreneur*?," I beamed.

"Yes," she chuckled. "Why do you seem so surprised?'

"I don't know...I guess you still seem so...*corporate* to me. If I may ask, what do you do?"

"Amongst other things, I'm a realtor in Malibu, Oxnard, Ventura, Ojai, and the surrounding area," she replied.

"Being a realtor takes so much confidence—especially in those locations," I stated in admiration. I was starting to feel as if I'd found a kindred spirit. "How did you overcome so much negativity? I mean...I haven't gone through anything like what you have, and yet I can't seem to get past my doubt. I feel like I'm going to fail before I even start. The mountain I have to climb seems so high."

"Two crucial things helped me. First, I knew I had to change if I wanted to be a productive, positive person. I set my feelings aside, retrained my brain, and got done what needed to be done. It took time for me to reach my subconscious, re-program my core beliefs, and counter my negative self-inflicted images with more positive ones. Second, I set tangible goals and did positive visualization in order to focus on my path and persevere until I attained my goals. I put my heart and soul into everything I did. Getting over my past trauma is a work-in-progress that I continue to practice to this day."

"Even now?"

"Of course! Everyone does to some extent. First you must acknowledge it. Then you can set it aside and bottle it up, so you can freely act on your current and future life. It doesn't happen overnight. Like I said, I've had so many do-overs I feel like I can start over from just about anything—except dying, of course. And the jury is still out on that one," she laughed.

"All of that sounds great," I said. "But it's easier said than done. It feels like sand slipping through my fingers. How does one 'bottle up' negativity?"

"I always tell people to find a passion. It replaces all of those negative thoughts. You have to *truly love* what you do. When you are totally consumed with your passion, you can't think about anything else."

When you are totally consumed with your passion, you can't think about anything else.
—Annie Evans

"What is your passion?"

"I have a passion for many things," she reflected. "But there is one that sticks out above the rest: *adventure*. I've lived a really adventurous life. You mentioned that what you're going through feels like you're about to climb a mountain. As it happens, when I was a child, I grew up exploring mountains. I spent a lot of time hiking in Monterey County and upper Carmel Valley. I've hiked down and back up the Grand Canyon. Nevada, among many other places. I even lived in Yosemite National Park for some years."

"Wow…"

"My sense of adventure has inspired me to travel and explore. I lived in Ireland for a while and, on my return, I fell in love with sailing. I had the great fortune of falling in love with a pilot who was building a boat. This passion for exploring led to my learning celestial navigation. There was no GPS in those days, and I logged 44,000 sea miles throughout the Pacific. I traveled up and down the California coast to Hawaii and back, down to Costa Rica, Panama and then over to French Polynesia…

"When I was working in the corporate world, I traveled the globe. I worked in several countries on a regular basis. I went to England, France, Germany, Spain, Switzerland, Italy, and Portugal. I traveled in Japan, Indonesia, Korea, the Philippines, Vietnam, Taiwan, Hong Kong, and even Cambodia."

"That's so amazing. But how does real estate fit in?"

"I see real estate as something of an adventure, too," she reflected. "Every area I represent features unique architecture, landscapes, and culture. In a way, I'm joining in with my clients on their adventure in a new home."

"Next!," the cashier shouted.

I couldn't believe the line had progressed, and it was finally my turn to pick up my prescription. Ironically, others were now waiting on me. I had become so engrossed in Annie's story and thinking about my passion for helping others that I could, at last, envision myself starting up that mountain. My doubts and negativity were still there, but they were losing their sting.

I hugged Annie and said, "Thank you so much. You have no idea how much you've inspired me."

"It's an honor to be part of your journey, Lynda," she said, sliding her business card in my hand. "If ever you need another boost to start up that mountain, give me a call."

MOMENTUM

Chapter Two

Living Life on Purpose

David (Dave) Blackford

I felt pumped after my conversation with Annie. The high I'd experienced from her guidance lasted for some time—until a day arrived that I'd dreaded for weeks: participation in my first charity golf tournament.

For most people, a golf tournament would be something to look forward to with excitement. For me, it was like facing a lion at the base of the mountain.

I'd had several professional golf lessons in preparation, to no avail. I whirled the club like a toddler swinging and missing at a baseball tee and landing on her rump. I was certain I was going to embarrass myself at this tournament, which seemed all the worse because I had a hunch several important people would be in attendance who might be beneficial to my business.

When I awoke early that morning, I had heart palpitations while envisioning what I thought was going to happen at the event. I pictured the club escaping from my hands as I took a swing; it swirled in the air and clunked a billionaire investor on his forehead.

I have to find a way to gracefully bow out of this tournament...

Deep down I knew I couldn't back out. I'd committed to something, and I had to keep my promise. Not to mention that it was for charity, after all...

I steeled myself and put on my brand-new golf shirt, shorts, and shoes. Before heading out the door, I grabbed a blueish visor I'd purchased for the occasion.

21

If nothing else, at least I'll look the part...

When I reached the golf club, I found myself surrounded by strangers. I had no idea who anyone was, but I doubted it would have made a difference. They all intimidated me to such an extent that I clammed up at the front desk.

"Excuse me?" I asked.

"What is your name?," repeated the woman behind the desk.

"L-l-l-l-ynda. Lynda Sunshine West," I replied.

The woman scanned a written list with a pencil and proclaimed, "Ah yes—here you are!"

She gave me some paperwork to fill out and processed my credit card. When the transaction was complete, she handed me a badge that had my name misspelled "Linda" without the *y*. I said nothing while forcing a smile.

"You are on team Blackford, right over there," she informed me.

I didn't see where she had been pointing, as I was too preoccupied with pinning my misspelled badge on my shirt. No matter how hard I tried, the thing hung lopsided. As soon as I finished, I asked: "Over where?"

"Right there," she gestured.

I had no idea where she was pointing; it seemed to be in the direction of a random gaggle of men and women laughing it up. They all appeared to be quite at ease with each other and eager to hit the green—or whatever the right expression is.

I still have time to duck out the door without anyone noticing... even though I've already paid.

From within the crowd, a kind-looking gentleman with white hair, well-groomed matching goatee, and steel blue eyes waved at me. My hands took over, gesturing back to him: "Who, me?"

He pointed his finger right at me; there was no mistaking it this time. "Yeah, *you*—come on. Let's get going!"

I should have escaped when I had the chance. Now it's too late.

I had no control over my legs as they delivered me to a group of total strangers.

The gentleman with the goatee cheerily extended his hand outward to me: "Welcome to team Blackford. I'm David Blackford. And you are—?"

"I'm L-l-l-l-ynda. Lynda Sunshine West," I responded, shaking his hand. Fingering the badge, I added: "Except this crooked thing spells it wrong. It's *Lynda* with a *y*."

"What a coincidence! I spell *David* with a *y*, too!"

"You do?"

"No, just kidding," he joked.

I felt like a gullible fool, but his wide smile made me feel at ease. "Nice to meet you, Lynda with a *y*. Come on, tee time."

He introduced me to the other two players, whose names I barely registered at that moment because I was too nervous about playing well to pay attention.

Janet and John. Or maybe Janice and George. Or...is he Paul? Well, whatever, I know it's the name of a Beatle—John, George, or Paul—but definitely not Ringo!

I trailed a half step behind the one person whose name I *did* know and tried to catch his attention. "Um, David?"

He turned his head back to say, "Call me Dave."

"Sure, Dave," I said. "Listen, I just want you to know...I don't know why I'm here. I don't know anyone here at all."

"Welcome to the club! I don't know anyone, either. I just met Janice and John here for the first time myself."

Janice and John! Now I'll make sure to know...

"What I mean is," I gulped, "I don't know why I'm here. I can't play golf at all. I'm terrible—a total liability. If I'm on your team, you are guaranteed to lose."

Janice, John, and Dave all chimed in at the same time to usher in support:

"Oh, don't worry about it..."

"We're just here for fun..."

"It's all about charity..."

"I'm not that great, either..."

I felt a little bit better now that it was out in the open and I had their support. When we reached the first hole, Dave grabbed a club and advanced toward the tee. He paused in front of me to say, "On second thought—I *am* concerned, Lynda with a *y*," he stated in a deep voice.

My heart throbbed.

Oh no, here it comes...

"You are?"

"But not about your golfing ability," he continued. "I'm concerned that twice you said you don't know why you're here."

He continued toward the hole.

"Wait, Dave," I called to him. "Of course, I know why we're here—it's for the charity...."

Dave ignored my statement as he marched to the tee. Everyone became silent as he drew his arms back to take what struck me as the perfect swing. We watched in awe as his ball soared through the air. It landed and rolled forward. It looked like a good shot, but I wasn't sure until Janice and John applauded.

"Beautiful," John praised.

"Excellent," Janice agreed.

While John and Janice each took their turns, Dave sidled up to me. "I know you realize this event is for charity," he said. "My concern is about something much deeper. I did a little research on you before coming here."

"You did?"

24

"Yes," he answered. "Based on everything I've read, seen, and heard, I think you have some work to do to be able to climb your mountain."

Did he say mountain*? How does he know about that?*

"Well, I'm only just getting started with the website and raising capital and—"

"I'm not talking about the details," he dismissed. "I'm talking about *purpose*."

With that, it was my turn at the tee. I grabbed a club and tried to remember everything my golf instructor had taught me. I felt all eyes upon me and shuddered.

Front foot slightly ahead of the ball...get close enough to the ball so that the middle of the club face reaches it with my arms out straight, but still relaxed...

I swung and made contact. To my astonishment, the ball went up in the air and straight—maybe fifty yards. But it was far and away the best shot I'd ever taken. The others applauded in acknowledgement. I hadn't embarrassed myself, after all.

We continued to play. My conversation with Dave resumed as we advanced from hole to hole. "What did you mean back there—about my not having *purpose*?" I asked.

"I'm sorry if I sounded critical, Lynda with a *y*," he reflected. "Many people struggle with identifying their *purpose*—it connects everything in our private and work lives. It gives meaning to whatever we do. If we don't have a specific purpose, our personal and professional lives become unfocused and we go around in circles. You need *purpose* to understand *why* you are climbing that mountain. When you have a rock-solid *purpose*, you have the foundation to be able to persevere and overcome whatever obstacles might come your way."

Many people struggle with identifying their purpose—it connects everything in our private and work lives. It gives meaning to whatever we do. If we don't have a specific purpose, our personal and professional lives become unfocused and we go around in circles. You need purpose *to understand* why *you are climbing that mountain.*
—Dave Blackford

"I never thought about it like that," I admitted. "How do you see your *purpose*?"

"In my case, I kind of relate *purpose* to *serving*. Whether you're focusing on the world collectively, a group of people, or even just one single person, you are living your life to *serve* that specific entity. I believe we're all on this planet to help one another. One of my favorite quotes is from Zig Ziglar: 'You can have everything in life you want, if you will just help other people get what they want.' My specific business purpose is to help as many people as I can."

In my case, I kind of relate purpose to serving. Whether you're focusing on the world collectively, a group of people, or even just one single person, you are living your life to serve that specific entity. I believe we're all on this planet to help one another.
—Dave Blackford

"People like me?"

"Yes, exactly," he chuckled.

My tensions eased with each progressive hole. The verbal back-and-forth with Dave took my mind off my lack of golfing ability, which was an eyesore compared to my teammates—but also a lot better than I thought it would be. They fed me words of encouragement when I swung and missed or smacked a line drive into the woods. It felt especially good when they jumped up and down excitedly after I sank a putt on the second try. "Now that I think about it, I am pretty good at mini golf," I remarked.

They laughed appreciatively. No one seemed to care that I was bogging the team down and probably in the vicinity of 30-something over par.

When we completed the course, we went back inside where we discovered our team had finished dead last in the contest. This meant we had to contribute the most to the charity. I expected my teammates to scowl at me with disapproval, since landing at rock bottom was entirely a result of my golfing ineptitude. They'd all played pretty well. Instead, they celebrated and toasted my game over mimosas.

"If I'd known we were supposed to have done badly in order to contribute more, I would have screwed up on purpose!" John shouted.

"Thank heaven for Lynda with a *y*!" Janice concurred.

"Three cheers to Lynda with a *y*!" Dave exclaimed.

After we swallowed back a few glasses, I realized I hadn't yet asked Dave about his business. He was happy to talk about it, although it involved a measure of personal sacrifice. "I had gotten full custody of my daughter when she was three," he said in a lowered tone. "It caused me to move away from doing some of the things that I had dreamed about. At that time, my *purpose* was to raise my daughter to the best of my ability. I was just going to work, coming home, and taking care of her. I focused on that for fifteen years. When she graduated high school, my father reached out to me and asked, 'Hey, do you want to start this business?' That's when everything started to click. Once again I started serving...."

Like Annie and me, Dave had left his "day job" to go off on his own as an entrepreneur. He founded Blacklock Designs as an umbrella name and a hub for his various products. He told me about A-Leg-Up®, a product created by his father that was designed to provide a stable and comfortable platform to perform such tasks as pedicures, trimming nails, putting on socks and shoes, and spraying foot powder or lotion. The device is useful for everyone, but is especially helpful for people who have hip, knee, or back problems.

"So, you see," Dave concluded. "Having a *purpose* is like having a powerful guiding force being with you all the time. Any time you question why you are doing something in spite of all the ups and downs, you must remind yourself of your *purpose*, and it gets you right back on your path up the mountain. But, as life circumstances change like what happened with my daughter, so might your *purpose*."

Having a purpose is like having a powerful guiding force being with you all the time. Any time you question why you are doing something in spite of all the ups and downs, you must remind yourself of your purpose, and it gets you right back on your path up the mountain.
—**Dave Blackford**

It was plain to see how Dave's philosophy, emotional story,

and living with *purpose* had enabled him to successfully serve and help people. As soon I arrived home from that wonderful event, I holed myself up in my office and jotted down all of my thoughts about *why* I believed I was embarking on my new career path. I spent hours scribbling down and crossing out ideas. I needed to hone in on my own exact *purpose* that would keep me motivated during all of those unexpected trials and tribulations. I knew I had to come up with my own personal guiding force that involved helping people in some way but was also distinct from Dave's—and everyone else's.

I woke up the next morning having fallen asleep on my notebook. I turned the pages and reviewed my chicken-scratch. Curiously, I hadn't written down a single thing about "getting rich" or "making money." That was part of the equation, for sure, but not my *purpose*. My eyes scanned down to the last lines on the final page…

<u>My Purpose</u>

To help women discover their value and learn how to share their voice with the world.

Nailed it!

Chapter Three

Imagining the Dream

Nadia Fleury

Now that my *purpose* was locked and loaded, I became eager to come up with creative ways to get started heading up the mountain. I realized how much I was benefiting from Annie and David's insights and now craved even more input from other experts, especially when it came to successfully visualizing what lay ahead.

I cleared my slate and enrolled in a five-day entrepreneurial event in Nevada where I could intermingle with people from a range of backgrounds and industries and learn from them. On the first day, I stepped inside a session with fifty other professionals and didn't know a single person.

The moderator of this session went on at length about what it takes to be a successful entrepreneur: courage and determination. I became mesmerized by her presentation and content—so much, in fact, that I began to feel somewhat more relaxed and comfortable around all of these other entrepreneurs. I didn't feel quite as out of place as I normally would and, for the first time, longed to make my presence known.

Then the moderator asked the group the following question: "Who in this room would like to come and sit in the *hot seat*, introduce yourself, and explain what you do in your business?"

Something about her statement gave me an itch to become even more engaged in the session. My mind began to spin. My heart raced. I felt perspiration seeping through my blouse.

I have to volunteer and share my business dream with the

31

group. Since I was able to measure up to Annie and David, I can rise to the occasion now.

Instead of just raising my hand, I leapt to my feet as if my seat were on fire to ensure no one else could intervene and get a word in ahead of me.

This is my moment. All eyes are on me. I want to be forthcoming and honest. I just need to be myself.

I took a breath, swallowed hard, and stepped in front of the room to take my place in the "hot seat" (which was actually a stool).

"You are very brave," the moderator acknowledged. "Tell us your name, what you do, and why you are so passionate about your business."

Here goes. My first time addressing a crowd. I deserve to be here. I am one of them.

"I am Lynda Sunshine West. I help driven women discover their value and learn how to share it with the world. I teach them how to show up as they are and not be afraid to do live videos. I started doing this because it took me fifty-one years to realize that I wasn't living—I simply existed. Before my mom passed away, she told me she had so many regrets. I decided I wasn't going to waste anymore of my time hiding and was going to live my life without any regrets. I've been on a quest to do so ever since she said those words to me."

The attendees soaked it all in. Some of them appeared shocked that I had the courage to stand up and share those words in public with a group of strangers. Even the moderator seemed momentarily thrown for a loop. She swerved back a half step before breaking out into a wide, appreciative smile. "That was brilliant," she raved. "I want to write that one down for myself!"

The moderator and the entire audience applauded.

I did it. I actually just spoke up in front of a group of strangers

*for the first time ever. Not only that, but they are responding well
to what I said.*

I sat down and reveled in the moment, my endorphins
refusing to settle down.

After the session, I was taken by surprise when one of the
entrepreneurs seemed to be vying for my attention. She had an
air of sophistication as she weaved through the crowd toward
me. She had brownish bangs on her forehead and wore a coral
designer blouse with elegant pearls around her neck. She waved
a magnificent, intricately designed purse unlike anything I'd
ever seen.

"I just have to speak with you," she said in what sounded
to me like a French accent. "I admire your guts and bravery."

"I admire your *purse*," I gaped. "Did you make it?"

"Why yes, I did," she answered, stunned that I had guessed
correctly. "Do you really like it that much?"

"Yes, it's gorgeous," I praised.

"Sold," she announced. "I'll give you one tomorrow—no
charge."

"No, you don't have to—"

She held up her hand to prevent my protest. "I promised
myself that if someone tells me she really likes the purse, I'd
give one to her for free."

"Thank you so much," I said, still unable to take my eyes
off that purse.

She extended her hand to me and said, "Nadia Fleury. So
nice to meet you."

I was able to distract enough of my attention away from the
purse to shake her hand. "Lynda Sunshine West."

"Wonderful to meet you, Lynda. Would you like to grab
something to drink and chat? We have some time before the
next session."

"I'd love to."

We went to the small café in the hotel and served ourselves beverages. We took two seats around an available table and started chatting right away as if we'd known each other for years. We exchanged information.

She informed me that she was originally from a small town in the province of Quebec, which explained her accent. She moved to California when she was twenty-four. Like me, she had quit her day job to fulfill her career dream as an entrepreneur. She had started out designing handbags such as the one she held in her hand and, a few years after that, she tapped into her chemist background and launched Avesence®, a successful skin care company.

"That is so impressive," I marveled, sipping my ice water. "But I have to ask—was there something in the beginning that sparked your imagination to get you going?"

"Now that you mention it, there *was* something," she considered. One day I started reading Napoleon Hill's *Think and Grow Rich*. I came upon the chapter where he wrote about imagination. I thought, 'Oh my God, *this is it*.'"

"What do you mean?"

"Well, Hill wrote that the key to capability is *imagination*. Once you use your imagination, you can create anything. I had thought that in order to create a product and run a business you had to *know* everything—but what did I really know? That was the turning point for me. I realized that I don't have to be an expert mechanic to drive a car. When I ran into a stumbling block in my business—something I didn't know—I could just try to creatively solve it, work around it, or think about someone I could hire or pay to fix it. Without that barrier of having to know everything, I became more open. I looked forward to experimenting with new ideas and became curious to find out what magic could be created."

"It seems like such a major leap to pivot from handbags to

cosmetics. Did you also tap into your imagination to accomplish that?"

"Yes, I did," she recalled. "But there is a story there. I was in my thirties and struggling to treat my oily skin. I went to a department store to find something that might help. I asked the nice lady behind the counter for some assistance and she suggested, 'For oily skin you can go to the Clinique counter over there.' I followed her to the Clinique line and, being a chemist, reviewed the ingredients of the products she suggested. 'These products have alcohol in them. They are also missing antioxidants that prevent the skin from aging. Maybe these creams work for young adults, but I'm in my 30s. I want more than an oil-control cream. I want something that would give me a radiant glow and protect my skin from pollution.'

"The clerk looked at me like I was from another planet. That's when I realized that not everybody sees what I see. The question hit me: 'Using my imagination, how can I solve my own oily skin problem using healthy ingredients that would also help my skin look radiant?'

"I gathered ingredients and started mixing things. I realized this was a lot easier for me than sewing handbags. I thought, 'Oh my God, I can do this all day long.' It no longer felt like work. It was *fun*. I thought of it like a quest. It gave me a reason to get up in the morning. I used my imagination to project the product into my mind from the consumer's perspective. I wanted to make it everything that a consumer would want— something that is easy to use and does it all."

"That is amazing," I said. "Was it smooth sailing after that or did you hit any roadblocks?"

"Are you kidding? It was *all* roadblocks," she chuckled, reflecting back. "But that was also part of the fun. I used my imagination from every possible aspect to break through those roadblocks. While I was dissecting the problem to the core, I would think to myself: 'What if I *could* do this? What would it look like?' I thought of using kaolin clay, which is an amazing ingredient for oily skin. Usually it is used in clay masks. You looked like a ghost until you washed it off.

"Then I imagined, 'What if I used the clay, but found a way for a consumer to apply it without looking like a ghost? What if it could actually stay on the skin? Could I possibly make such a formulation?'

"I imagined that the clay could be invisible, stay on the skin, and still be effective. It took two years of research and development to make it happen, but I finally did it. It worked. Using my imagination changed my life."

I looked down at my cup. Deep down I doubted my imagination was large enough or that I had the capability of fulfilling it.

"What's going on?" Nadia asked. "Tell me."

"I...don't know," I hesitated. "Sometimes I just think of my real self as being too hidden and buried to be able to imagine and accomplish my dream."

"What are you talking about? That woman I just saw in there who marched in front of the room determined to tell her story doesn't strike me as someone who hides from anything. You've *already* put yourself out there. I recognize a leader when I see one. All that said, I know doing something new takes some getting used to. It's not easy to stretch our comfort zone. Trust me when I say you are doing it well."

"You make it sound like I'm the Cowardly Lion from *The Wizard of Oz* who was afraid of everything but had the courage inside all along." I mused.

"Yes, you are!" she shouted, leaning forward. "You already have what it takes inside. Before you climb up your mountain, you need to imagine yourself already having reached the top. Hiding is the opposite of freedom."

Before you climb up your mountain, you need to imagine yourself already having reached the top.
—Nadia Fleury

"I believe you," I said. "But every time I start imagining the end result of my business, I instead picture how my last business venture lost $70,000…and then my mind goes dark."

"I will share something with you," she said in confidence. "Our mind is often preoccupied with assessing what we might lose or what we don't have instead of what we might gain. I learned a trick when I was a child. My family was poor and everything we had was either second-hand or a hand-me-down. My cousins made me feel I was lacking because I didn't have beautiful things. One day, instead of dwelling on what I couldn't change, I imagined I had a magic wand that I used to make everything around me beautiful. I still do this. When I am imagining my dreams coming to fruition, I focus on the magic wand making it happen for me. This way, I keep thinking from a place of success rather worrying about the possible failures. Everything boils down to your thoughts and feelings."

"I can't wait to try that," I considered.

"In your case, all you need to do is focus your magic wand on the image of that person in that session who bravely stood up and spoke. That woman—meaning *you*—can accomplish *anything*!"

* * *

That evening, as soon as I entered my hotel room, I sat at the edge of the bed and closed my eyes. I tried to block out all past failure in order to conjure up images of creating training videos for and with women. I envisioned a live video with a couple of hundred women tuned in. I pictured myself looking

37

confidently into the camera, offering practical advice and words of encouragement to other women based on my knowledge and experiences.

Then a bat fluttered across the screen...and another...and another...until it became a flurry of creatures filling my head and screeching at me that this was just another venture doomed to lose money and fail.

At first, I hid from the bats. But then I remembered everything Nadia had said to me earlier that day. In my mind's eye I grabbed a magic wand, cast it around the bats, and willed them to vanish. Before they could return, I homed in on the image of myself settling into my seat after having spoken up during the session earlier that day. I remembered how it had electrified my body knowing that I had the capability to be so articulate and confident.

With those positive images and sensations swirling in my head, I was able to cast the wand again to flip channels: first to my successful videos; next to the engaged expressions of the women with whom I was interacting and helping; and, lastly, to my bank statements, which showed ballooned earnings and savings each month. Just before I opened my eyes, I saw myself gaining momentum climbing up to the top of that mountain....

* * *

The next morning, I couldn't wait to find Nadia and tell her what had happened. I looked around in the hotel restaurant and spotted her sitting at a table looking at a menu. I approached her from behind, fully prepared to thank her for having offered so much wisdom.

Before I could speak, Nadia turned around in her chair and presented me with a brand-new handbag, just like the one she carried. Here I was—about to thank her for the precious advice she had given me—and she was the one gifting me.

I was so touched by her thoughtfulness I could hardly speak. "I...I don't know what to say. Thank you so much, Nadia. I will treasure it."

"My pleasure," she said, gesturing for me to take a seat.

"I can tell by the eager grin on your face that you have something exciting to share with me," she surmised.

"You guessed right," I replied.

"I would love to hear all about it over breakfast...once our food arrives, so we won't be interrupted," she grinned.

We ordered and enjoyed our breakfasts the moment the waiter plunked the plates in front of us. I wiped my lips with a napkin and recounted my experience from the prior evening—bats and all. "I can't wait to do the exact same thing again," I declared.

Nadia's expression turned serious. "May I suggest something, Lynda?"

I stared at her with a blank expression.

"To create something new, it's important to stay in your awareness. When you start doing the same thing, it becomes a fixed habit. Over time, the habit creates the same thing. In order to bring new experiences, it's good if you don't do it exactly the same way," she recommended. "In order to stay creatively free, try something different. Listen to music. Or, first take a relaxing bath," she suggested. "Nothing new gets created from the past. If you want to create *new experiences*, something truly unique and special, it must originate from the future...."

Nothing new gets created from the past. If you want to create new experiences, *something truly unique and special, it must originate from the future.*
—Nadia Fleury

MOMENTUM

Nadia and I continued our wonderful conversation for another two hours. We became so engrossed we lost track of time and even missed a workshop session.

When we finally placed our tips on the table and packed up to leave, I experienced an *Aha!* moment. Thanks to Nadia, I had come up with a catch phrase of my own:

Always looking forward.

Chapter Four

Taking Little Steps

Krysten Maracle

I spent the next several weeks *moving forward*. I worked non-stop, round-the-clock to get my business off the ground. I had everything mapped out, written down, and organized, but I hadn't anticipated all of the details I would have to manage and the fires needing to be put out along the way. Time management became a huge issue for me. I was inhaling my own fumes. The only breaks I took were to practice visualization, as Nadia had coached me.

One day, the massive number of tasks became too much for me to handle. My video productions were behind schedule, my website was filled with bugs, and I was struggling to pull together the agenda for my first client event. It seemed like people only communicated with me when they needed to dump bad news—major delays, things not working, expenses going over-budget, bills remaining unpaid, and so on.

Desperate to clear my head, I meandered around the streets of Point Loma, San Diego, for a long time. I turned onto Catalina Boulevard and became aware of a few storefronts, including Peet's Coffee and Jensen's Foods. I was starting to feel a bit dehydrated and tired, so I wandered into Peet's Coffee. I believed it would be the best place to sit for a few minutes, rest, and collect my thoughts with a cup of comforting kid's hot chocolate (with extra whipped cream). It also seemed like the least expensive option available; I had enough cash flow issues without adding extravagant hot chocolate expenses

41

on top of it.

I nearly changed my mind as soon as I entered the coffee shop. The line was pretty long and there were no chairs available. Everyone was seated solo at tables intended for two to four people. They all seemed hyper-focused on their phones, iPads, and laptops; many had earphones or headphones on. I'm not exactly the type to sit with complete strangers and interrupt whatever they happen to be engrossed in. Even though I had spoken up at the event where I met Nadia, I still had a terrible fear of meeting new people.

Before I could change my mind and exit, the line started to move. The woman in front of me told me to order ahead of her, since she was waiting on someone anyway. I ordered my child-sized hot chocolate—which is not as scalding as the adult drink—paid, and almost instantly received my cup from the smirking barista, who was evidently entertained by my having requested such a wimpy beverage. It was as if I'd asked for a glass of skim milk at a seedy bar filled with whiskey-drinking bikers. I considered excusing myself by lying that it was for a little kid and not me, but then thought the better of getting into a pissing match with a barista. Besides, I couldn't wait to slurp down my wimpy drink.

Basking in the aroma of the hot chocolate, I skipped away from the counter. Before I knew what was happening, my foot became tangled in a large shopping bag next to a table. I tried to steady the hot chocolate, but it was too late; the brownish liquid splashed onto the back of a woman with straight long blonde hair who was involved on her laptop. As fate would have it, she was wearing a white blouse. My immediate concern, however, was that she had been burned—even though a kid's hot chocolate could hardly inflict such damage.

"Are you all right? I'm so sorry!" I cawed, grabbing whatever napkins I could find from a table nearby.

42

The mass of blonde hair swirled around. I was fully prepared for a verbal lashing from this stranger, but something shocking happened instead. The woman was smiling from ear-to-ear—*laughing*, in fact. I'd never seen so many white teeth. Her complexion featured a beautiful reddish tan. "Oh, it's nothing. Don't worry about it. I hardly feel it."

I feverishly dabbed the napkins against her back to soak up the stain on her blouse. "But your blouse—"

"It's fine—at least you didn't get my laptop," she chuckled with a vibrato that seemed to shake the room.

I opened my purse and extracted some bills, which I presented to her. "No, it's not. This stain isn't ever going to come out. Here, take this—you can buy a new blouse."

She moved my hand away. "Nonsense. Keep the money."

She pulled back her chair in order to reel in her overloaded shopping bag. "Actually, this was *my fault*. I left my gigantic bag blocking the middle of the aisle."

She yanked a brand-new pair of shiny black scuba flippers out of the bag. "Anybody would trip on these things."

"You like to go scuba diving?" I asked.

"Yes, it's *so good*," she beamed. "One of my favorite activities. I love the water and boating.... Listen, you can stop blotting my back. It's fine, really."

I paused, doubting that it was in any way "fine." But her smile continued to put me at ease. I felt guilty, though, and didn't know what to do. I still held about half a cup of kid's hot chocolate; I longed to salvage what I could and enjoy at least *some of it*. I looked around for an available table, but there wasn't one to be found. I was about to make an excuse along the lines of being in a rush to the smiling woman, but she gestured to the empty chair at her table. "You look tired and could use a break. How about having a seat with me?"

"I don't know..."

"Please," she insisted. "I usually dislike socializing, but I feel like we have a bond. My name is Krysten Maracle."

"Miracle?"

"No *Maracle*—with an *a*, not an *i*. Someday, I'll explain it to you," she laughed. "And my first name is spelled with a *y* and not an *i*."

With that statement I was compelled to take a seat. The coincidence of name spelling was too much for me to handle while standing. Maybe we really did have some sort of bond? "I'm Lynda Sunshine West. Lynda is spelled with a *y*."

"How about that!" she giggled. "What do you do, Lynda?"

"I'm just starting my business," I revealed. "But it's not going well. It's like I'm heading up this mountain and not making enough progress to get going, much less gain any momentum."

"Interesting," Krysten considered. "I'm far from a business expert, but I do have an observation—if you don't mind."

"Go on."

"I could tell you were in a major rush when you walked in," she reflected. "I'm not blaming you for the hot chocolate spill—but I could tell without even looking that you were kind of hopping around while anxiously looking for a table."

"Yes," I admitted. "Although I would describe what I did as *skipping*. I admit it, I'm a pretty impatient person."

"Here's an idea," she suggested, sipping from her cup which seemed to contain some form of espresso with cream. "Oh, that is *so good*!"

Krysten's reaction to her drink was contagious. I gulped a mouthful of hot chocolate and made an "mmm" sound. "Mine, too."

"Where was I? Oh yes—instead of hurrying, rushing, and skipping everywhere, why not try *little steps* to getting things done."

"Little steps?"

"Let me explain," she said, her mind adjusting. "You may not believe it by looking at me, but I work at the Navy Information Warfare Center, the NIWC—at least that's what they call it today. It could change tomorrow."

She laughed yet again. I couldn't help but join her.

"What do you do there?"

"It's complicated—and I'm not allowed to reveal everything. If I do, I'll have to dispose of you…" She let out a hearty laugh and continued, "But let's just say I do Navy contracts…"

Krysten could tell I still didn't get it, so she continued: "In simpler terms, I work in Naval cyber-security."

Naval cyber-security! That sounds so important. This woman is amazing. Who knew this smiling, laughing woman with scuba flippers and an espresso could be involved in such a thrilling day job?

"Wow."

"Don't be so impressed, it's not like the movies," she snickered. "Don't get me wrong, I love my job and I've been doing it for a really long time, but it's mostly sitting at a desk all day—except when I have to travel. Anyway, I didn't mention my job to brag—most of it would seem pretty boring and unglamorous to you, anyway—but I want to help you find a way to get up that mountain without tripping."

Annie. David. Nadia. Each one had something remarkable to offer me. Maybe Krysten does as well?

"Frankly, I can use all the help I can get!"

"Great—this will be *so good*, trust me," she began, lit up with excitement. "In my job I work as a decoder and programmer. I install software. In the Navy, each and every project is a huge task. You have to imagine that for every five lines of code there are maybe 50,000 procedures that have to be followed. If I don't follow every single one, the whole thing gets blown and

I have to start all over again."

"Ugh," I reacted.

"That's the least of it for me," she confided, drawing me in closer. "As it happens, I'm dyslexic, so it makes it ten times harder for me to make sure everything is done right and by the book."

Now I'm truly tripped up. How can she perform such a daunting, detail-oriented job with dyslexia?

"Okay, I can tell by your expression that either you are confused or don't believe me," Krysten observed. "You're wondering how I have the ability to code and program software with dyslexia."

"No, it's not that at all—"

"It's okay. I know, it's hard to believe. But it's what I do every single day," she chortled. "When I first found out I had dyslexia, I couldn't pronounce it and certainly couldn't spell it. But it explained a lot about me. I couldn't comprehend things and was forced to repeat the eighth grade. I felt ashamed. People said I was 'dumb' and 'illiterate.' Numbers and words would constantly get jumbled up in my head. Once I was aware of this, I became determined to prove everybody wrong. Not only did I finally get through eighth grade, I made honors in the ninth, tenth, eleventh, and twelfth grades. All of my hard work paid off tenfold!

"I also learned how to compensate and take precautions. I became even more cautious and precise than most people. If I can do it, so can you. We're obviously both *action people*. But when we run blind and fast all the time, we tend to trip and make a lot of mistakes. In order for you to get up your hill, you need to break your major projects down into little steps. This way you're not racing to get through a task. You make fewer errors because you're not competing to catch up with anyone else.

"Part of a successful project management routine is to create subroutines—little steps along the way that you can complete and check off. It feels *so good* to check off a task as being done—even a little one. I don't even think about the next step until the current one is done and flawless—or at least as close to perfect as I can get it."

Part of a successful project management routine is to create subroutines—little steps along the way that you can complete and check off. It feels so good *to check off a task as being done—even a little one.*
—Krysten Maracle

"I don't have to rush and skip important steps. I don't have to hurry up to the top of the mountain. If I do, I'm just going to keep tripping, falling backwards, and spending all of my time repairing my mistakes and putting out fires."

"That is fantastic, I love it," I said, downing the last drops of my hot chocolate. "You have no idea how much you've helped me. I'm glad I wandered in here and tripped on your flippers."

"Really? Ha—that is *so good*!" she exclaimed. "In my job I work by myself most of the time. It's nice to interact with someone and realize I have something to offer."

"You have *tons* to offer, Krysten," I countered. "Look at everything you've accomplished—even with dyslexia!"

"Oh, that's the least of it," she laughed. "You should also know that I was the only blonde girl who received a computer science degree at San Diego State University in 1987!"

MOMENTUM

48

Part Two

Touching Down on the Top

Wise Man #2 - Dr. Greg Reid

Call it whatever you want: residual income, passive income, progressive passive income, or even lazy income. Any way you look at this strategy, it means one simple thing: *receiving money for doing next to nothing.*

Residual income, which is mentioned in *Wealth Made Easy*, means you set up your business model once and then get paid for it forever. It ends up being that surprise check that shows up in the mail when you need it most. It often feels like *gravy* or *free money*. It is one of the easiest, most effective ways of gaining momentum while you are climbing to the top of your business mountain.

Need an example? How about this: a membership model, such as at a gym, in which customers sign up and pay an upfront annual fee to join and then an additional set amount every month. That money shows up in your account every four weeks. What work did you have to do after the customer signed up? Absolutely nothing.

Need another example? Buy a gumball machine for about $750 and stick it in a mall. Buy colorful gumballs for a penny apiece and then charge a quarter for each one. The gumball replacement process is on autopilot, which means you get twenty-four cents profit on every gumball without having to do a single thing.

Many entrepreneurs struggle because they don't have access to hearing about simple gold nuggets like residual income. If you want to receive more pearls of wisdom, do these simple things:

1. Network to meet smart, accomplished people who have already succeeded at what you are trying to do.

2. Join a mastermind of even smarter, more accomplished people.

3. *Ask* these smart, accomplished people for advice! Do not be afraid or intimidated. They are human beings just like you and probably had help from experts along the way to achieve their successes. Many of them truly enjoy sharing their wisdom with others.

4. Fake it until you make it. Pretend you are already at the top of the mountain you are climbing. It's unlikely anyone will think to question whether you deserve to be there or not. If anyone is ever condescending to you, it signals that he or she doesn't deserve your respect or attention anyway.

Last but certainly not least: Believe that you *deserve* to be queen or king of that mountain. You are only *Three Feet from Gold*. With this mindset, you will create a unique realm of your own that attracts success and builds continuous momentum.

In these next chapters, as you arrive at the top of the mountain, you will be greeted by these champions: *Paige Panzarello, Amy Burton*, and *Annie Evans*.

Chapter Five

Connecting with "the Cashflow Chick"

Paige Panzarello

My knees shook as I sat in the bank with my husband and waited for our turn to meet with Mr. Steele, the branch loan officer. We were in the process of taking a loan out to buy a new house, and I was nervous about our financial situation— both personally and for my business. Although I was making money, it seemed as if my cash flow was never going to normalize. Some months were great, while others were lousy. The unpredictable nature of incoming revenue was driving me crazy. Yet here we were—applying for a homeowner's loan.

What are we thinking?

My husband, whom I affectionately call "Wheatie," placed his hand on one of my knees to calm down my shaking. It worked to some extent, at least; that knee remained still, although the other one kept right on bouncing.

To distract myself, I stood up and stepped over to the water cooler. I filled the cone-shaped cup with cold water. After I gulped it down, a container filled with 100 Grand chocolate bars on the counter caught my eye. I grabbed one, unwrapped it, and gnarled off a piece with my incisors. As I chewed and savored the taste of chocolate, caramel, and rice, I couldn't help but overhear the middle of the cheerful conversation that was taking place between Mr. Steele and his female customer on the other side of the wall.

"Are you kidding? I love coming here to the bank. Every

time I do it means I am making more money and helping more people!" the woman exclaimed.

"Funny, I've heard people refer to *you* as the bank," a deep, resonant voice followed—probably Mr. Steele.

"Yes, that's true," the woman chuckled. "I do love being the bank!"

"Well, since that's the case, I'm honored that you chose *this bank* to do all of your banking and wire transfers. Thank you so much, Mrs. Panzarello."

There was something about she said and how she said it that intrigued me. I just had to speak with her when the pair stepped out of Mr. Steele's office. My husband jumped out of his seat in anticipation to shake hands with our banker—a tall, slender black man in his 50s who wore a magnificent gray suit and burgundy tie with dark-framed glasses.

Wheatie seemed stunned when, instead of acknowledging Mr. Steele, I addressed the gorgeous woman standing beside him. She had the waviest, silkiest long blonde hair I'd ever seen, with green eyes and a striking profile. "I'm sorry if I'm being presumptuous, but I have a question for you—Mrs. Panzarello, is it?"

Her face lit up with a wide smile, and her hand reached out to me for a handshake. "Yes, but please, call me Paige." Sliding the remainder of the 100 Grand bar in my other hand, I returned the handshake and stated, "Nice to meet you, Paige. I'm Lynda Sunshine West."

I turned to my banker: "Great to see you, Mr. Steele, I don't mean to be rude…I just need a couple of minutes with Paige, if that's okay."

"All right, Mrs. West," Mr. Steele nodded. "I can get started with your husband in the meantime."

"Wheatie," I said to my husband. "It'll only be a minute, I promise."

The two men shrugged at each other and headed into Mr. Steele's office.

Paige seemed amused by my exchanges with the men as she said, "Wonderful to meet you as well, Lynda. How may I be of service to you?"

"Well, I have to be honest," I admitted. "I inadvertently overheard the end of your conversation with Mr. Steele. Nothing confidential...."

"Oh, don't worry about it," she dismissed. "We were just shooting the breeze anyway at that point."

"I heard what you said about 'being the bank.' What did you mean by that? Are you a financial advisor of some kind?"

"No, not exactly," she replied, noticing my disappointed expression. "But I do know a thing or two about money—and I love teaching people. Is there something specific I can help you with?"

"Well, what is it that you do if you aren't an advisor? You see, I'm an entrepreneur and could use some advice."

"How much time do you have?" she laughed. "I don't want you to keep your husband and Mr. Steele waiting too long!"

"Don't worry about that," I dismissed. "They have plenty to do before I go in there and sign my life away."

"Okay...how do I explain it," she ruminated. "I'm known as the Cashflow Chick. I help people build wealth through note investing."

I chomped on another bite of the chocolate bar and gulped it down as I contemplated her moniker. "The Cashflow Chick—I love it! How did you come up with it?"

"I wanted something memorable that explains what I help people do. At first, I didn't like the 'Chick' part. Everyone who knows me will tell you that I am not a 'Chick' the way they used to refer to women back in the 1950s. A friend said to me, 'Paige, you have the unique opportunity to redefine what *chick* means.' I took that to heart and the Cashflow Chick was born."

"How lucky I am to be connecting with you. You'll have to explain to me what 'note investing' is, though. I've never heard of it."

"Most people haven't," she said. "In simple terms, instead of buying houses, I buy the debt that is secured by the house. In other words, I buy mortgages. That makes me the lender, which is what you overheard me tell Mr. Steele. Once I become the bank by buying the mortgage, I am entitled to receive payments from the borrower. My niche is that I invest in a mortgage when the borrower has stopped paying. These notes are called 'non-performing,' and my goal is to try and help people stay in their homes by working with them to start paying again. Life happens to each of us every day, and most of my borrowers have had life happen to them—divorce, medical issues, job loss, and so on—that's why they stopped paying their mortgages. It doesn't make them bad people. It's just life. I try to give people a second chance. The best part is I get to make great money passively while helping people!"

"That's so cool," I marveled. "You must do very well."

"Yes—but not always!" she blurted. "I lost $20 million in the recession of 2007 back when I was doing a lot of real estate construction."

"$20 million—Holy Moly!"

"You said it," Paige concurred. "I started back in 1996. My business really took off and grew very fast in 2002. Things were rocking and rolling. I had thirty-six employees in my construction company and I was making money hand over fist.

"When the recession hit in 2007, I thought I was going to be okay—at first. I wasn't over-leveraged. The problem is, people owed *me* money and couldn't pay—they went bankrupt. Then I had to come up with ways to pay back what I owed to other people. It took three years, but I was determined to make things right.

"I liquidated everything I owned at rock bottom prices—even taking losses—and managed to pay *everyone*. I knew I was doing the right thing. Personal integrity is so important to me. I did not consider my loss as a failure, but rather chose to look at it as a 'very difficult learning experience.' And I did learn from it! I'll tell you, it shaped me as the person and investor I am today.

"After the crash, I entered a completely different medium as an entrepreneur and started to slowly regrow my wealth. I gradually went back into real estate, but not to 'fix it and flip it.' I realized that wasn't for me anymore. I created a whole business around note investing, and I love it. I can do it anywhere in the world as long as I have a phone and the Internet. It's not location specific. It offers a freedom in my life I never had before."

"How does cash flow fit it in?"

"I am going to tell you what should be the two favorite words of every entrepreneur: *passive income*."

"Ah," I acknowledged. "I've heard of it."

"I *love* passive income. It's like making money in your sleep. The best part about passive income is that you don't have to be actively involved on a day-to-day basis, and you aren't trading time for money like when you have a 9-5 job. You create a business model and implement it. Usually your participation is in the beginning to put the deal in place. Once you do, you 'set it and forget it.' Other people handle the day-to-day for you, and you go to the mailbox to collect your passive income, which I like to call 'mailbox money,'" Paige explained. "Tell me, Lynda, *what's your what?*"

> *The best part about passive income is that you don't have to be actively involved on a day-to-day basis, and you aren't trading time for money like when you have a 9-5 job. You create a business model and implement it. Usually your participation is in the beginning to put the deal in place. Once you do, you "set it and forget it." Other people handle the day-to-day for you, and you go to the mailbox to collect your passive income, which I like to call "mailbox money."*
> **—Paige Panzarello**

"I'm sorry—I didn't catch that. It sounds like an Abbott and Costello routine."

Paige's smile widened. "Most people ask the question, *what is your why?* But it's not that at all. You need to be asking yourself, *what is your what?* In other words, *what* is your immediate need at the moment? Do you need chunks of cash or streams of monthly cash flow? Do you need to supplement your income for retirement—or do you just need extra 'play' money? Are you looking to hold something long-term or short-term? Defining your *what* will guide your path. And, your *what* may change as you grow as an investor, so it is important to revisit it every once in a while."

"Well," I considered, "I have a podcast called 'Women Action Takers Podcast' and I do video work that empowers women."

"Excellent—that sounds like fun!" Paige exclaimed. "There are so many things you can do with that business to create passive income."

"There are?" I blinked in fascination.

"I assume you personally spend time in the mastermind, so

that wouldn't be passive income—but you can create monthly or quarterly subscriptions or memberships to receive your videos and podcasts," she suggested.

"Will people really pay on a regular basis for that?"

"Absolutely," Paige responded. "Of course, you need to have the right pricing model and *add value* to the package, so people feel as if they are getting something extra by signing up for the subscription or membership. Another thing you can do through your podcasts is align yourself with products or businesses and services you like. By promoting them, you can earn passive income from affiliate fees."

"My mind is racing with excitement," I said. "I have so many wonderful ideas in my head to create passive income and gain momentum to get up the rest of my steep mountain. No wonder they call you the Cashflow Chick! You are truly amazing."

"I try," she said with a modest tilt of her head.

My husband chose that opportune moment to poke his head out of Mr. Steele's office and wave me in. "Looks like my time is up," I informed her. "But I have to thank you for your time and all the great advice. Here is my card if you ever need a favor from me."

She produced her own card from her purse and clenched it in my hand. "Don't feel as if you owe me, Lynda. It was truly my pleasure being of service to you. Like I said, I enjoy teaching and helping people to become financially free. I want you to contact me if you need anything else. But also contact me if you don't—I want to hear how things turn out!"

"You bet," I agreed, giving her a massive hug. I snatched a 100 Grand bar from the container and handed it to her. "Thank you so much, Paige. What you just gave me is worth *at least* a hundred grand!"

"*Yum*—I love these," she said, hugging me back. "Good luck, Lynda!"

Chapter Six

Following the Ask Method

Amy Burton

As I entered the beautiful hotel in Uptown Charlotte, North Carolina, to attend a three-day conference, I had no idea who was going to be there or what lessons I might learn. I felt in my heart it was going to be an amazing experience and was more than ready for it. I'd traveled across the country for this particular event and hoped to get my business to the next level by gaining some face-to-face exposure with entrepreneurs on the east coast.

I was primed to do as many red-carpet interviews with like-minded speakers and attendees as possible for my show. I was stationed on the second floor at the top of a grand winding staircase: the perfect location for everyone to see what I was doing. I proudly waved copies of my book *The Year of Fears* at visitors as they flooded the conference hall. I latched on to some remarkable entrepreneurs who eagerly agreed to be recorded on my show.

During some down time, I was able to sit back and reflect on the past few years. I felt so proud of myself for having come such a long way in my personal life and career.

Yet, as confident as I was, occasionally the old fears crept back in. I would stare down my mountain and wonder what the future had in store for me below. I was learning to shove those feelings away by stepping into the fear with my newfound courage. I was growing increasingly comfortable settling into my role as a red-carpet interviewer at these live entrepreneurial

59

events.

Early in the afternoon, two interesting looking women emerged from the winding staircase. Something about them intrigued me as they headed straight toward registration. They must have known they were late to the conference, yet didn't seem the least bit stressed. They were cheerful and poised as they chattered and giggled their way past me: one, a stunning woman dressed in black with dark, upswept hair and catlike eyes; the other, a spunky, blazing redhead. They glanced my way, smiled, and waved in unison. As the dark-haired woman eyed my stack of books, I overheard her say, "Oh, I love books! We must stop by this table on the way out!"

The redhead nodded with delight.

Hours later, as the conference drew to a close, I glimpsed the same two women rounding the corner on their way out. They headed straight for my table, displaying the same level of enthusiasm.

These southerners sure are happy people!

The dark-haired woman extended her hand to introduce herself: "Hi, I'm Amy Burton, and this is my friend, Rachel Gilmore. It's so nice to meet you, Lynda!"

How does she know my name? And why is she addressing me like an old friend?

It was as if she were reading the question on my mind as she continued, "I see your name and beautiful face on your book cover. How exciting, Lynda! Please, do tell. We want to hear all about it."

Before I could open my mouth to reply, Rachel reached her hand to greet me and echoed, "Hi Lynda, it's wonderful to meet you. Yes, please, do tell!"

Following our introductions, I told them a bit about my book and what I do for a living. I explained that I was in Charlotte filming live red-carpet interviews with conference speakers and attendees.

Rachel's eyes lit up: She was ready for the camera to roll! Before I could utter another word, she leapt at the chance to schedule an interview.

Amy, on the other hand, shook her head as if to say, "No way, not me!"

I certainly wasn't going to pressure her into filming if she was uncomfortable. Still, I was intrigued enough to ask: "What do you do for a living, Amy?"

Her eyes sparkled with excitement. "I own Revel Salon and Color Studio, a small salon and spa company just across the state line in Lake Wylie, South Carolina."

Rachel chimed in as if her friend hadn't been standing right there. "Don't let her fool you—Amy's business isn't any old 'small-town salon and spa company'! She's an amazing businesswoman who has accomplished much more than she's leading you to believe. She's an extremely intuitive entrepreneur."

"Well," I said, shifting back to Amy. "In that case, maybe you'll reconsider being filmed?"

"No thanks," she demurred. "I'm boring anyway."

"*Boring*! Another understatement," Rachel contradicted. "What *she* thinks is uninteresting, *I* always find to be fascinating. It seems anything Amy wants in life, regardless of the naysayers or obstacles that stand in her way, she does what it takes to make it happen. If you don't believe me, spend a few minutes with her and you'll understand what I'm talking about. I've heard story after story of how she speaks her truth, steps out on faith—then poof! With a wave of her magic wand, things fall right in place."

Rachel shifted to Amy and continued, "Go ahead and tell her how you do it, Little Miss Queen of Questions!" She turned back to me to add, "I call her that because she always asks a lot of questions. She'll be the first to admit she credits much of her success to *asking*."

"Okay, Amy," I smirked. "I'll *ask*: How do you do it? What's your secret?"

Amy glanced down at the table. Clearly, she disliked tooting her own horn.

"Well, yes, I've grown the company quite a bit since I opened—but the truth is, I'm just getting started. I have so much more to do. As Rachel said, I ask a lot of questions. So much so, I suppose, it can be irritating to some people—especially those who settle for mediocrity in life and in business."

She threw her head back and laughed.

"Frankly, I don't care. I don't make any apologies for my endless inquiries. With everything I have planned for the future, I'm going to keep asking! You see, Lynda, I must rely on the people who have gone before me to help pave the way. You know what they say: 'Why reinvent the wheel when someone has already done what you may be dreaming of doing yourself?' The golden path of least resistance is sometimes the most obvious, yet the least seen.

"We allow the fear of looking foolish or ignorant hold us back from seeing what's already right in front of us. All you have to do is muster up the courage and ask someone else how she did it—then give it a whirl yourself. I'm telling you—it works like magic!"

"What an interesting approach," I considered. "Maybe I need to be asking more questions myself. I mean...I ask questions when I interview people. I just don't ask them things that might benefit *my business and me*."

I tensed up as I pictured myself doing just that. Asking successful people questions solely for the purpose of improving my livelihood seemed presumptuous.

What if someone gets mad? What if I make assumptions and

overstep my bounds with the wrong person?

I've always disliked confrontation. Every time I questioned things as a little kid I was scolded and told to keep quiet.

I feel like a frightened five-year-old girl again.

"Listen, Lynda, I know we just met, but I'm going to be straight with you. It's obvious by the title of your book that you've worked hard to overcome a lot of fears in your life. I completely relate. I understand how childhood events—even seemingly harmless ones—can form the foundation for limiting beliefs that carry over into adulthood. But holding onto fear—especially fear of asking questions—isn't serving you…is it, Lynda?"

I bit my lip: a telltale giveaway that she had my number.

She saved me the trouble of saying it outright. "I understand where you're coming from. Sometimes I feel afraid, too. But if I allowed myself to focus too long on negative things, I would be too terrified to make my next move. Forging ahead, pushing through the fear is what's gotten me this far in business.

"If you take only one tiny bit of advice from me, I would tell you the first step to getting anything in life is to *ask, ask, ask*! That's how you build momentum and get ahead.

"Now, putting aside asking questions for a moment, what I'm deeply passionate about is growing and serving people. I can sense you're the same way. People like us believe everyone can tap into hidden greatness with the proper tools and the knowledge of how to use them effectively. Success is not as difficult as people think it is. If I can do it, anyone can."

How impressive—so much vision and enthusiasm coming from a hairdresser! This woman is obviously not your run-of-the-mill stylist.

"I love your passion and excitement, Amy! I wish I had more time to learn more about your business philosophy and future plans."

"Absolutely—if you don't mind my rambling. Let's make

plans to chat a bit later," she suggested. "Right now, you and Rachel need to get her interview scheduled. In the meantime, I'm fine stepping aside to read your book, if that's okay."

While Amy thumbed through my book, Rachel and I went over the details of her upcoming interview. We also got to know each other as she filled me in on her transformational travel company, and I opened up about a few of the hurdles I was facing in my business.

Rachel was jolted by an idea. She stepped over to Amy, interrupting her reading. They had a brief, animated discussion and then marched back to me.

"We talked it over. I'd like to take you out to dinner with my group," Amy invited.

"Me? Really?"

"Yes, *you*," Amy stated. "I think we may be able to help each other."

I was dumbfounded.

We've only just met and she wants to treat me to dinner?

"You look puzzled," Rachel observed. "You shouldn't be. There's so much the two of you can learn from each other."

I wasn't joking when I said Amy is humble. She totally underplayed what she's accomplished. She built her company from the ground up, having had no experience managing employees or running a company beyond being a solo entrepreneur. She started up in the middle of the recession after having lost a good paying job in the drapery industry. She took a huge risk that most people wouldn't remotely consider.

Despite having very little money and numerous people telling her she would never make it, she pressed on while believing she had a higher purpose in life. She wants to make a difference helping others feel beautiful on the inside, as well as on the outside. In fact, when you walk in the door at Revel, the first thing you'll notice is a plaque on the wall that says:

Create a life that
FEELS GOOD
on the inside.
Not one that just
LOOKS GOOD
on the outside.

"There are so many things you can learn from Amy about how she runs her business. The service providers are the best team of professionals I've ever seen. The culture isn't catty or cutthroat, or snooty and uncomfortable, like some salons and spas can be. What never fails to surprise me is the energy and atmosphere. The employees never compete with each other. Amy's company is a teaching salon and spa. She typically hires people who are new to the industry. She coaches and grooms them from day one. She teaches them how to be *business professionals who provide beauty services*, rather than *beauty professionals in business*. Her employees are truly happy and *love* working there. You feel the energy the instant you walk in the door. They treat every guest like royalty."

"Guest?" I chuckled. "Is it a hotel, too?"

"No, silly. They refer to their clientele as *guests* because that's how they treat each person—as a *guest*, not a number, like some places do. You see, it's not just about the beauty services they offer. It's an uplifting, beauty *experience*. Everyone leaves there feeling beautiful, inside and out. Time and again, Amy credits her success to having the courage to *ask* for help whenever she needs anything—"

"Okay, okay, I get it—you've sold me on dinner!" I relented, addressing Amy: "But what on earth can I impart to you?"

"I'm enjoying what I've read of your book so far," Amy praised. "As it happens, I'm writing my first book now. It's a bit intimidating, being my first project and all. I'm kind of winging it and could use a little advice. In fact, I would love the opportunity to pick your brain a little…if you don't mind me asking a few questions!"

"I told you—she's an *asker!*" Rachel winked.

* * *

We made plans for dinner the following evening. Our reservation at a local Brazilian steakhouse included Amy, Rachel, and Sean Douglas, one of the amazing conference speakers.

I gasped when I stepped inside the restaurant: I couldn't believe Amy had invited me to such an extravagant—and expensive—place. At the time, I was unaware that she typically eats only plant-based foods. Meanwhile, she had chosen a meat lover's haven for our feast! I hadn't met a vegan who would be open-minded enough to take her friends to a steakhouse.

The interior of the restaurant was aglow in transcendent orange. The hardwood floors soaked up the color and reflected the atmospheric lighting in all the right spots. A phenomenal salad bar was situated in the middle of the main dining area. After we filled and emptied our salad plates, waiters came around with delicious carved meats: roasted chicken, sirloin, sausage, ribs…yum!

What have I done to deserve this?

Midway into the delectable feast, Amy and I got down to business. We homed in on how I'd worked so hard to finally reach the top of a mountain that I once thought was impossible to climb. I had a *real* business with *real* clients—and now I wanted to gain momentum, expand, and make some *real* money. The moment I stared downhill, however, I was still held back by lingering fear. "I guess deep down I'm petrified of getting to that next level," I sighed. "What if I can't handle it? What if I'm not good enough?"

"Not good enough? Don't be ridiculous," Amy dismissed. "But I'm glad you were confident enough to *ask* the questions—that's a start! To gain momentum and succeed in business, you must decide what you want and then *ask, ask, ask*! What I mean is: *Ask* yourself first, listen to your heart, and then follow your intuition. Most people already know what to do after that. Often, they are too afraid of taking action because it involves the risk of being vulnerable. That's where *the ask* comes in. Once you've decided what you want, then you need to seek expert counsel and *ask* your questions. Don't ever think about whether it's dumb or how the other person might react. *Just ask*. What's the worst that can happen?"

"I don't know," I mulled over. "Embarrassment... humiliation... being put in my place as an amateur."

"Get those thoughts right out of your head," Amy ordered. "You must tell your inner voice over and over again that you are worthy. You deserve to be in the company of this other person. You are an equal."

"Easier said than done," I sighed. "Maybe it would help if you shared one of your *ask* stories?"

"Seriously, Lynda, I could write an entire book series featuring all of my *ask* stories. I have asked for everything at one time or another—from a better rate on my credit card, to complimentary upgrades, to business advice, you name it! There are so many, I may have to take you out for dinner again tomorrow evening to cover even half of them."

"Maybe you can just give me the highlights?"

"You got it," Amy nodded, drinking some ice water to clear her throat. "Think of *asking* as a way of gaining momentum in business and in life. You can even call it *The Ask Method*, if you like. It's all about having the courage and inner confidence to *ask*

67

the right questions of the right people to get what you want or need—especially when you're feeling stuck. Sometimes it means being *tenacious.*"

"*Tenacious*," I repeated, enjoying saying it aloud. "I'm tracking 100% with you, Amy."

"So here goes, my first story," she began. "Before I opened my salon and spa company, I searched the Internet for other businesses that seemed similar to what I had envisioned. I started with companies that carried the products I was considering. I also made sure to look far enough outside my local area to keep people from being skeptical of my intentions. After a few phone calls, I chose a salon and spa in a city about two hours south of Lake Wylie. It just happened to be where my parents were living.

"Being so far away from the area while conducting research, I felt confident that my inquiry wouldn't upset the business owner I was targeting. I made a phone call and asked to speak to the owner. When she came on the phone, I proposed taking her to dinner so I might have an opportunity to *ask* a few questions about how she started her company. She accepted my invitation, and the rest is history! From that point on, my new friend referred me to a group of salon and spa coaches who helped me organize and design the basic structure of the business. Every step of the way, as my company grows, I continue to *ask* other experts who have gone before me. I've never been turned down, insulted, or embarrassed—not once."

I soaked it all in, longing to be as courageous as her and *ask* my questions of the right people.

"Can you share another example?" I asked.

"I think we have time for one more," she stated. "A few years ago, I was stuck at the top of my mountain, just like you. I was charging ahead at lightning speed when, all of a sudden, I became so stressed out I could feel burnout knocking down my door. I was exhausted and terrified. I was sure I was going to crash at the bottom."

"What did you do?" I asked.

"The only thing I knew how to do," she replied. "I *asked* and *asked*…and then spent the next few years transforming my life. I changed everything from my diet to my mindset. It didn't take long for me to realize how important self-care is—especially for anyone desiring to create, sustain, and grow a successful business—and also live a long, happy life. I became immersed in the teachings of amazing transformational leaders, studying under the Success Principles Master himself: Jack Canfield. I'm now a Certified Success Principles Trainer, using all of his incredible wisdom to thrive both personally and professionally. Had I not *asked*, none of it would have happened and I wouldn't be where I am today."

"I love it."

"Tell me, Lynda: Is there anyone you admire in business? Someone you wish you could spend more time with and learn from?"

"Why, yes—several, as a matter of fact."

"For now, suppose you could only pick one."

"There's one specific person who comes to mind," I considered. "He offered me some guidance when I was working on my book. His name is Dr. Greg Reid. I met him a few years ago when he was speaking at an event. He's someone I really admire. He's positive, upbeat, and energetic. He always seems to get what he wants in life. I don't know how he does what he does. I wish I knew his secret."

"Terrific! How do you feel about calling him and *asking* for a favor?"

"Well, I suppose I could," I deliberated. "He's a busy guy, though. I wouldn't want to bother him."

"There you go—making excuses!" Amy pointed out. "You have no idea what he's doing now or if he's busy. You're creating a barrier to convince yourself not to dial his number. If he doesn't answer, you leave a message. If he answers and says he can't talk right now, *ask* him when might be convenient."

Amy snapped her fingers across the table. "Do me a favor. Take out your phone."

"Now?"

"Yes, *now*," she ordered. "Don't even think about it. Just press Greg's number and *ask* if you can hang out with him for a few days to study what he does and how he does it."

"I don't know, that sounds like a pretty big request. He'll think I'm a stalker!"

"Nonsense," Amy shot back. "You're making excuses again. You don't have a clue what he's thinking. To be fair, though, you want to acknowledge that his time is valuable. You can offer to work for him in exchange for the opportunity to watch him in action. I don't know Greg, but I bet you'll be surprised by his answer."

"Go ahead," she prodded. "Do it. *Asking* is free, and there is freedom in *asking*! Trust me, you'll feel empowered—even if you don't get the outcome you want. Each time you *ask* it gets easier and easier until it becomes part of what you do. I have to remind myself that we are all on a wonderful journey of self-discovery. We must be open to *asking*—to both giving and receiving. We are all teaching and learning from each other. Those who are truly successful in life remember where they started and want to give back. Most of us are willing to mentor those traveling the road we've already been down.

Asking is free, and there is freedom in *asking*.
—**Amy Burton**

"As you start your descent down that mountain of yours, *ask, ask, ask*! Just *ask* Greg and then do the same with other experts. *Ask* them whatever your heart desires. Be brave… be bold… be who you are meant to be! The only stupid questions are the ones not asked. Ask every question from a position of fearlessness, strength, and confidence. Believe in yourself, you are a fellow traveler. Believe you are their equal and that you *deserve* to be there with them and hear their answers."

The only stupid questions are the ones not asked. Ask every question from a position of fearlessness, strength, and confidence. Believe in yourself, you are a fellow traveler. Believe you are their equal and that you deserve to be there with them and hear their answers.
—Amy Burton

"If you ask for something and the person responds, 'No,' simply say, 'Next!' Always remember: Some will be accommodating, some won't. Either way, so what? Someone else is waiting to help you! Your time as a caterpillar is ancient history. Your wings are waiting. You've got this, Lynda—go for it, girl!"

For the first time ever, I was able to look down to the bottom of the mountain without any fear whatsoever. I was gaining momentum. I could see my wings—strong and beautiful—as I started to soar.

I pressed Dr. Reid's number on my phone. He answered on the first ring. I heard his familiar no-nonsense voice: "Hey Lynda—what's up, champion?"

Geronimo!

MOMENTUM

Chapter Seven

Acting **As If...***When Achieving a Goal*

Annie Evans

I was riding high for some time after my dinner with Amy and the phone conversation she'd prompted me to have with Dr. Reid. I ended up spending several days shadowing and learning from him. In exchange for this privilege and the benefit of his time and wisdom, I helped his team set up various events. As I've told him on more than one occasion, I think I ended up with the better end of this arrangement.

Now that I had become comfortable with "the Ask Method" and had come a long way to overcoming my fear, I longed to put everything I learned into practice and start zooming down that mountain. My goal was to play with the "big boys and girls" and develop even higher-profile business relationships to double—if not *triple*—my business. In spite of the fact that I had a real business and was making money—including some residual income, thanks to advice from the Cashflow Chick—I continued to feel like I was still stuck at "the kids' table."

How will I ever graduate to the big time? Will I ever feel like I am truly worthy and at the same level as other successful entrepreneurs? Will I always feel like an amateur?

By sheer coincidence, something caught my eye at the corner of my desk. I picked it up: the business card from Annie Evans, my friend from the drugstore line who had helped me combat negative thoughts. I reflected back on my conversation with her and her open-ended invitation to call her anytime I needed "another boost up the mountain."

As it happened, I didn't need a "boost up," but rather, "a boost *down*" to double my speed down the slope like a professional skier. Somehow—given my newfound confidence with the *Ask Method*—I didn't think Annie would mind this distinction. I wondered what she would think of everything that I had accomplished since our brief encounter, and if she had any advice that would help me finally be able to join the "adults' table."

I dialed her number. It rang only a couple of times before a familiar voice picked up: "Hello?"

It struck me that both Dr. Reid and now Annie answered their phones. I had been finding that, while phones are in use 24/7 for texting, Googling, emailing, social media, apps, calendars, selfies, and on and on, hardly anyone actually used the devices for their intended purpose: *speaking to other people*. I really appreciated that these great people took the time to continue to answer their phones, whether they knew who was on the other end or not. I tucked this piece of information away for further reference, vowing to answer the phone whenever possible (except if it's spam, of course).

"Is this Annie?" I asked.

"Yes, who is this?"

"It's Lynda," I replied. "Lynda Sunshine West…we met at—"

"Oh yes!" she exclaimed. "The entrepreneur at the drugstore. I somehow had an odd feeling you would be contacting me today. How is your business? Do you feel you have gained momentum up the hill?"

"Yes, I have—everything is just great!" I touted. "Things are going really well—in part because you were so helpful to me in overcoming negative feelings."

"How *wonderful*," Annie chimed.

"In fact, things are going so well I thought you might be

helpful to me in terms of accelerating and gaining momentum *down* the hill."

Annie didn't hesitate to respond: "Absolutely, I'd love to help—let's chat in person."

"In person? I'd love to," I said. "Are you sure you can spare the time?"

"For you, Lynda, the answer will always be *yes*."

* * *

We agreed to meet in front of a bookstore; not just any old one, but one that had a large café with comfortable seating where we could sit and talk as long as we liked. Both of us arrived at the same time, welcoming each other with big smiles and open arms for a warm hug.

Annie seemed even more ebullient than during our first encounter. After our usual "you look amazing" pleasantries, she anxiously gestured to the store's entrance. "Let's go inside. I'd like to show you something before we order drinks and sit down."

I followed her through the revolving doors and past the stacks of new releases and table promotions.

Where is she leading me?

We turned down the Self-Help/Inspiration aisle, whereupon she started thumbing through several spines. I supposed she was searching for a book she thought might be helpful for continuing my journey.

After a few seconds she found what she was looking for, yanking a paperback off the shelf and presenting it to me with delight. "Look!"

I glanced at the glowing cover of *Live for a New Day: No Matter How Bad Today Is, There is Always a New Day.* The orange design featured a sailboat heading toward a spectacular burst of radiant white light. "What a gorgeous book," I reacted before finally realizing something important: *Her name appeared at the bottom.* "Oh my goodness! This is *your* book—

congratulations, Annie! It's *beautiful*."

I couldn't resist hugging her again. "If I buy this copy will you autograph it?"

"Of course," Annie grinned. "But, frankly, I could just give you one for free...."

"No, I want to buy it," I insisted. "You deserve the purchase and the royalty. Besides, if I buy it, the store will have to stock another copy."

I brought the book up to the register. After I stepped away with my purchase I gushed to Annie, "I can't wait to read it. It looks so inspirational."

"I do hope you enjoy it," she said, waving me toward the café. "Come. Enough of my shameless plug. Let's get our drinks and grab a table, so I can hear about your business developments."

We made small talk while on line at the café. When it came to my turn, I ordered my usual hot chocolate and Annie followed with a request for her favorite latte. She insisted on paying for mine with her store app, but I wouldn't allow it. If anything, I felt that I should pay for her, given all the wise advice she had already imparted to me.

"Nonsense," she dismissed. "It's just a hot chocolate. You'll get it next time. Besides, I have so much on my account from gift cards. It would be my pleasure to share."

"Okay," I reluctantly conceded. I didn't want her to think I was unappreciative or still struggling, but her transaction happened too rapidly for me to do anything further about it.

At the least I had bought her book....

We grabbed our drinks at the other end of the counter and maneuvered our way around several occupied tables. This time, I made extra certain not to trip and spill my hot chocolate!

After a brief search, we claimed two available cushioned chairs with a coffee table. "Perfect!" I declared.

"Yes," Annie agreed. "This will do."

Once we were situated, Annie prompted me to fill her in on everything that had transpired with my business since we last met. I told her about all of my successes, largely thanks to the amazing advice from her and so many other people like her.

"So...what is the problem?" Annie asked. "It sounds like you have made sensational progress."

"It's not a problem, exactly," I said, struggling to come up with the right words. "In spite of everything I've accomplished, I somehow can't gain momentum and speed down the hill. I love my current clientele, but I would love to have a few recognizable celebrity names come into my business. But somehow, I don't think they would be interested in paying attention to me. It's like I'm an adult who is still sitting at the kids' table and I'm not recognized as the expert I feel that I am becoming. It's like I am someone who doesn't deserve to get to that next level. I just don't know how to approach 'the elite' without somehow feeling like I'm less accomplished than they are and undeserving of their attention and business."

Annie sipped her coffee as she thoughtfully contemplated my words. I slurped my hot chocolate and waited for her to respond as the seconds ticked by. "I'm sorry, I was babbling," I blurted. "You must think I'm just a big baby."

"No, no—not at all," she countered, touching my hand. "I was actually thinking how smart you are to be so aware of what you are experiencing. I'm actually quite impressed."

"Thank you," I said.

"As it happens, I have the ideal solution for you. You know the expression 'Fake it 'til you make it'?"

"Yes, of course."

"Well, this is an improvement of that expression," Annie stated. "You need to act '*as if.*'"

"*As if...* what?"

"I know it sounds funny, but it's just *act as if,*" she explained.

Annie could tell I was intrigued but somewhat confused, which is where she seemed to hope I would be.

She continued: "I believe that, when opportunity knocks, you should be ready to step up and literally 'fake it until you make it.' In other words, you are acting *as if* you *truly deserve and are worthy* to be in the presence of these so-called celebrity businesspeople. You need to be behaving *as if* you already have many, many connections at their level. Trust me: No one will ever doubt or even question you about it. You are signaling to everyone that you are already at the adults' table which, frankly, is where I believe you are sitting anyway."

...when opportunity knocks, you should be ready to step up and literally 'fake it until you make it.' In other words, you are acting as if *you truly* deserve and are worthy *to be in the presence of these so-called celebrity businesspeople.*
—Annie Evans

"That sounds amazing," I absorbed. "Though somehow it feels like I would be pretending to be someone I'm not—like I'm being dishonest."

"Don't be silly," she argued. "Let's put it this way: Do you feel you have the same confidence and expertise as when you originally started up your mountain?"

"No," I chuckled. "Looking back, I kind of feel like that was a whole other person."

"Exactly," she pointed out. "You are doing the same thing now by shedding your current skin to become the next iteration of the person you will ultimately become."

"Wow, I never thought of it that way," I reflected. "Have you ever acted *as if?*"

"Yes, a few times," she admitted. "On one occasion, I was hired to be a liaison for a sporting goods company. I really thought that it was an admin job, but on the first assignment they sent me from California all the way to Colorado. I walked in the front door of Pearl Izumi, the sports apparel company, and I was met by about ten people—all of whom were department managers. They had been waiting for me to arrive with anticipation. Mind you, I had no experience in sporting goods or product development/manufacturing whatsoever— zero, zilch, *nada.*

"American Sports Group, the company I worked for at the time, had been hired to 'turn the company around.' I knew I had to step up big time and find some way to prove that I could make a difference. I spent months flying back and forth to Colorado. Over time, I was able to help guide the company to develop and produce its largest season ever—despite the fact that it was severely underwater and had despondent employees, computer Y2000 issues, overpriced sourcing, and some financial limitations. Not only was I able to command cooperation from all departments, I created a workaround for the Y2000 issue and rewrote and updated their vendor manuals."

"But...how did you accomplish all of that?"

"Funny you should ask!" she laughed. "The CEO at the time asked me the same
question. He'd seen the total lack of productivity and poor response from the whole team who had all been just letting their work pile up on their desks. It became so bad that it became common knowledge employees were interviewing with other companies during lunch breaks. All of that changed because I was able to turn things around.

"I admit it: I didn't know a single thing about this business when I first started. Like I said, I had absolutely no experience in this industry whatsoever. I am entirely self-taught and proud of it. I proceeded to *act as if I was an expert authority*. I faked it the entire time I was in Colorado. I must have done a great job faking it because they all listened to me, trusted me, and followed my instructions. Everything worked beyond my wildest expectations. Every day I was 'faking' it less and less. It changed my life and I made lasting friends.

"After that, I had more confidence about my abilities—except now I'd officially 'made it.' I'd proven to myself and others what I *could do*. From that point on, I wasn't shy about stepping up and acting *as if* whenever the need arose, which of course it did. I had to stand up to some 5,000 Korean and Chinese factory workers and the business leaders and tell them what they needed to correct and replace. Imagine…culturally speaking, they weren't used to hearing criticism and direction from a woman 'back in the day!'"

"I get it now," I said, adding with conviction: "I'll *do it*! I'll act *as if* the very next time it's needed."

"Fantastic," Annie cheered, toasting me with her coffee cup. "You are officially at the adults' table. Of course, you're like Dorothy in *The Wizard of Oz*. You've had the power within you all along and didn't know it!"

I raised my hot chocolate cup, tipping it against hers. "There's no place like home, Annie…."

We laughed, downing the contents of our cups. I placed my recent purchase on her lap and handed her a pen. "Sign away, oh great and powerful author!"

Annie slapped her knee. "Oh, yes, you reminded me of one more thing. I acted *as if* when it came to writing my book. I didn't know *anything* about being an author and publishing a book."

"How funny, Annie. Now that you mention it, I did the same exact thing with my book!"

MOMENTUM

Part Three

Maximum Momentum

Wise Man #3 – Frank Shankwitz

I'm a cowboy at heart. When I was younger, I loved motorcycles and rode one for many years as an officer. I know what having real momentum—whether it's on a bike or in terms of achieving your life dreams—feels like physically and emotionally: Both can give you a major adrenaline rush.

There are a few things you have to know when you're accelerating and gaining speed. First, you're going to come crashing down if you aren't authentic—your true self. You can't pretend to be someone you're not or else people will see right through you and not trust you.

If you want to keep going faster and faster, you have put your authentic self out there and get out of your comfort zone. In business, that often means public speaking, which can be pretty hard and scary. When I started to do public speaking, I used little note cards.

One time I was about to speak at a gala. A lady grabbed the notes right out of my hand and tore them up right in front of me.

I panicked and asked, "What are you doing? How am I supposed to speak without my notes?"

"Frank," she said. "You don't need them. You speak from the heart. You know what you're talking about."

Since then, I stopped using notes and that lesson stuck with me: Always speak from the heart. If you do that, people will feel your natural charisma and will always be on your side when you're on stage.

I've also learned that you can't gain maximum speed without collaborating well with others. There are ups and downs on every team and you'll certainly have clashes along the way. We had our share of challenges making *Wish Man*, the film about my life and how I co-founded the Make-A-Wish® Foundation, but it all came together because everyone shared a common goal and worked well as a team.

My deepest wish is for you to zoom down your personal highway with wings on your feet—in police motorcycle talk we call this symbol "the Winged Wheel"—and that you land speedily, successfully, and safely at the finish line.

I couldn't have wished for better people to help you on your journey down the mountain like *Sohaila Handelsman*, *Mike Packman*, and *Dennis Haber*.

Chapter Eight

Being Authentic

Sohaila Handelsman

At long last, my client list was expanding and my business model was sustaining itself. I was beginning to generate revenue and profit. Acting *as if* was enabling me to put myself out there in front of people in a way that I never thought possible. I was confident enough to not only engage with top entrepreneurs, business professionals, and celebrities at every level, I also felt like I deserved to sit at the adults' table with all of these notables. In fact, I was starting to believe that I had become *one* of them.

My descent down the mountain had officially begun! I was accelerating with the wind behind my back. The ground beneath my feet felt smooth and steady. I was gaining *momentum.*

Now that I had some success under my belt, I felt that I deserved a break. The timing couldn't have been better that week when a couple of close friends, Tricia and Kate, invited me to join them for a girl's night out. I was promised a night of great food, scrumptious desserts, and laughs. Little did I know what was in store for us as we stepped inside the storefront....

Hardwood floors. Mirrored walls. Red curtains. The exotic sounds of Middle Eastern music. A couple of women dressed in tights stretched out their hamstrings on the rail like ballet dancers.

I burst into a cold sweat. One of my worst fears was being realized.

"A *dance studio*?! No way!" I protested, already feeling myself shrinking back down. "I am *not* taking a dance lesson—

85

not ever!"

"Oh, come on, Lynda, relax—it'll be fine," Tricia comforted me.

"Just try it out," Kate followed. "If you really don't like it, I'm sure you can stand on the sidelines."

My friends, seemingly prepared for my reaction, lured me forward. The intense fear shooting up and down my spine reminded me of my first time going into the dentist's office when I was a little girl. "No...please...I don't want to..."

I imagined myself trying to do dance moves and looking like a total fool. I pictured myself twisting and turning out of step from the others, tripping on my left feet, and landing on my butt.

I was a bit relieved when I spotted three to four more women—not dressed in any kind of dance garb—hovering by a table off to the side. They sipped wine, popped grapes, and ate cheese and crackers while enjoying their conversations.

Maybe a couple of these women are like me and don't want to participate. I can just hang out with them, eat some good cheese, and watch. If that doesn't work, maybe I can fake an ankle injury....

Tricia and Kate led me to the food and drink table and introduced me to the other women: Nancy, Fern, Hillary, and Samantha. We exchanged introductions and pleasantries when Nancy blurted, "Oh, I can't wait to hit the dance floor! I've been looking forward to this all week."

I cringed.

"I hope we learn some belly dancing," Samantha said, bouncing her hips. "I've always wanted to learn how to do that."

Of course Samantha did. I guessed she was thirty years old at most and had a tight, shapely body like Britney Spears in her prime.

"I can't wait to meet Sohaila," Fern chimed in. "I hear she's been dancing since she was a child—something like forty years."

"She's absolutely gorgeous," Nancy raved.

"And so talented," Hillary added. "She's danced all around the world—Dubai, Syria, Paris, Israel. She's performed on major stages and even in front of sheiks. Something like 90% of her students have moved on to become professional dancers with dance companies or have become teachers themselves. A few of them have won major dance contests."

"Wow," everyone gushed.

Although my stomach was churning, I had to keep busy with something, so I stuffed a couple of grapes in my mouth.

"She does dance fitness—I think it's called NewVo. The 'Vo' part is short for 'vogue,'" Hillary stated.

The women shouted words and phrases in unison like "Cool!" and "How clever!"

"She also runs a 'sensual woman' program," Nancy informed us.

"*Oooh*," the women leered, causing me to nearly choke on a grape.

"I want to do that, too!" Samantha volunteered.

I felt woozy, like I might pass out. Tricia and Kate stood right by my shoulders, propping me up. There was no chickening out.

We stood at attention as the volume of the music went up several decibels. When it reached a crescendo, the lights flashed, red velvety curtains in the back of the room parted, and out sprang a magnificent sight. A breathtakingly beautiful, buxom woman with lengthy auburn hair shimmied her hips in front of us to the accompaniment of a Middle Eastern-sounding song. She wore a tank top with wraparound, jangly objects around her waist that produced tambourine-like sounds. Out of thin air, she produced a partially see-through silk orange veil, which billowed in the air.

All of the women—including me—gaped at the sight of this majestic, graceful woman. We clapped, cheered, and *woot wooted* as she slinked across the dance floor. Although there were no men in the room, I could only imagine how they would have responded to the sight of this sexy and talented belly dancer.

She performed with a beaming smile for several more minutes, finishing with a flourish and holding her pose as the music stopped and the lights returned to normal. We applauded and whistled with appreciation. She curtsied and mouthed the words "Thank you."

She gestured for us to stop, and we gradually simmered down. "Thank you so much for coming. Welcome to my studio. If you haven't already guessed, I am Sohaila—your hostess for the evening."

Sohaila seemed to float across the dance floor as she continued to speak. Her smile never abandoned her face. Although she couldn't seem to keep still, she somehow found a way to make eye contact with each one of us. I could feel her energy fill up the room. It all seemed so...*natural*.

"We are going to try a few simple things," she said. "And have lots of fun.... We'll break free of the monotony of life for a few hours. As you tap into your five senses, you will feel empowered...perhaps *sensual* as well."

A few of the women giggled. I could see Sohaila's eyes track me as I cowered behind my two friends.

She resumed addressing the entire room; fortunately, she didn't seem to be directing her comments specifically at me. "There is no need to be shy. This is a *safe space*. I would like all of you to feel relaxed and at home. This is a place where you can be yourself. *You can just be who you are*. No one will judge you. As you get to know me, you will find that 'what you see is what you get.' There are no pretenses. I believe in being authentic at all times."

88

Being Authentic—Sohaila Handelsman

Uh oh. There's that word: 'authentic.' What does that mean for me? I came in so confident and now, in a matter of minutes, I've turned to Jell-O. Have I reverted backwards? Is this my true form? Here I've been acting as if *and finding success. Have I been deluding myself? Does this mean I'm 'acting' too much and not being 'authentic'?*

Just my luck...I'm going to be put on the spot and embarrassed by the one belly dancer who, apparently, can see right through me.

"Any questions before we begin?"

Yeah. Like...when can I go home?

"I have one," Kate called out.

Great. One of my friends has to ask a question. Now everyone is staring at me because I'm hiding behind her.

"Go ahead," Sohaila directed.

"How did you get your name?"

"Ah, what a wonderful question!" she exclaimed with her hands clasped. "When I was very young, one of my teachers was once helping me change into my dance costume. She casually referred to me as *Sohaila*—and it somehow stuck. Later, I found out that it has Persian origins and means 'a star in the sky.' There was also once a famous dancer with that name."

The group murmured approvingly.

I love her name. The only thing special about mine is the y *in it.*

"Okay, ladies," she called out. "I would like each of you to find a place on the dance floor—it doesn't matter where. We are going to try something very simple."

Without any hesitation, all of the women—including my friends—obeyed her command. No one seemed to suffer from insecurity like I did. I lagged behind. Exposed. I stood there like an abandoned sheep.

Oh, God. I can't do this. Why did I let them con me into

coming here?

It dawned on me that it would be far worse to be singled out as a sheep than to go out on the dance floor and face the music, as it were. I dragged my limp body to the dance floor, maneuvering to a place at the end where I hoped no one would notice me.

"Wonderful," Sohaila said, once everyone was in place.

The lights dimmed and music began to fill the room. To my surprise, we didn't hear blaring sounds from Morocco or any exotic places like that. Instead, the notes were gentle and soothing, the kind you might hear while getting a relaxing massage.

"Now take a deep breath," she instructed. "Hold it for a moment...then slowly exhale."

Breathing: I can do that. Easy-peasy—I do it all the time!

I breathed in and out several times along with the slow rhythm of the music. Before I knew it, I was already feeling more relaxed.

Sohaila's voice lowered as she said, "Close your eyes... continue to breathe..."

What is this—dance or meditation?

"I would like you to experience all of your senses...the sound of the music...my voice...the feeling of your breaths going through your body...."

Wait...maybe she is trying to hypnotize us?

"Now...with your eyes closed and continuing to breathe deeply...imagine you are someplace else...on a dance floor at a party...at the beach...by the ocean...in a forest...back on vacation...wherever you like...."

Her prompt was even easier to follow than I thought it would be. Within seconds I found myself transported onto a beach.

I feel the sand beneath my feet... smell the ocean air...hear the waves crashing against the shore...see the magnificent sun rays beating down from the sky...I can feel the cool breeze....

Sohaila's voice blended into my beautiful new landscape: "Allow your senses to come into play and take over your body. Let them direct how you would like to move...."

I'm swaying back-and-forth...now I'm skipping across the sand...dancing through the waves...this feels wonderful...I've never felt so alive!

We continued like this for some time with several more prompts before Sohaila guided us to return to the room and slowly open our eyes. I couldn't believe it: I had moved to a completely different spot on the dance floor. Glancing around, I noticed that everyone had moved somewhere else—and they were equally as astonished.

Sohaila applauded each and every one of us. "That was beautiful dancing! I've never seen such excellent movement!"

Danced? Did I just dance?

"Where were you during that time? How did you feel?"

By this time, I felt so relaxed that when Sohaila taught us a few belly dancing moves I didn't feel in any way self-conscious about trying them out. While I knew I would never go public with this, I didn't think I looked so bad seeing myself wiggle and jiggle in the mirror reflection. I was actually a touch disappointed when the session ended.

* * *

A half hour or so later, I found myself flitting from one person to the next, giddily conversing about our dance experience. We shared a few personal stories—and some business cards, as well.

All of a sudden, I was approached by Sohaila herself. She looked even more magnificent up close with her widened smile.

She promised not to be critical...I hope I didn't look like a fool.

"Lynda, right?" she asked.

"Y-y-yes," I stammered.

"I thoroughly enjoyed your dancing," she praised. "You looked quite poised."

"Really?" I blinked. "Come on, you're just messing with me."

"Never," she contradicted, looking me straight in the eye. "I don't ever lie. Like I said earlier, 'what you see is what you get.'"

She seemed so convincing that it was impossible for me to doubt anything she might say. I had such an instant trust that I whispered, "May I ask you something…a bit private?"

"Oh?" she grinned.

I presumed her expression meant she thought I was going to inquire about the sensual dancing. "It's not anything like what you might be thinking," I chuckled as we moved a few feet away from the other ladies.

"How may I help you?"

"Something has been troubling me," I said.

"Go ahead…"

"A brilliant, dear friend recommended a technique called acting *as if* to help me feel equal to people who are more accomplished than I am so I could approach them. It's kind of like 'fake it until you make it.' It's cool how you shared that you are authentic. I sometimes feel like I may be inauthentic by acting *as if*."

"Has it worked for you?"

"Oh, yes—very much so," I said. "I'm finally starting to feel like my business is gaining some momentum…."

"Wonderful!" she said, bouncing in place. Sohaila was truly a person who couldn't resist being in constant movement. "What is troubling you, then?"

"How do I recognize when I'm pretending too much? You know…being a phony," I explained.

"Lynda, the fact that you are concerned about this at all

signals to me that it doesn't seem possible for you to ever be any kind of phony," she stated.

"But...I've been pretending that I'm more successful than I really am to some wealthy people in order to feel like I deserve their attention and business. Is that wrong of me?"

"I understand your concern," Sohaila considered. "But the fact is, you become as successful as you *feel*. If you portray yourself the way you truly feel, then the extra attention you receive is *deserved*. No one can ever deny you your feelings.

"It is true that, in order for you to be authentic, you must always be who you are. You have to be *real*. You never want to lie to anyone, take credit for things you haven't done, or pretend to be someone else. On the other hand, the amount in your bank account is of no concern. Your measure of 'success' may be different from someone else's, but so what? If you *feel* successful, you *are* successful."

In order for you to be authentic, you must always be who you are. You have to be real. *You never want to lie to anyone, take credit for things you haven't done, or pretend to be someone else. On the other hand, the amount in your bank account is of no concern. Your measure of 'success' may be different from someone else's, but so what? If you* feel *successful, you* are *successful.*
—Sohaila Handelsman

"Listen carefully to me, Lynda. I've danced and taught dance for many years. I obviously never have to act *as if* at all when it comes to my craft. But I'm also an entrepreneur, a

93

business professional. I've created this dance studio all by myself. I've even started my own program called CEO Women. Guess what? I never went to business school. I never even took an accounting class. I had to act *as if* myself in business on several occasions. But look around. I'm living my dream, doing what I love."

"You are so wonderful, Sohaila," I raved. "You've made me feel a lot better. I'm really glad I came tonight."

"Thank you for coming," she responded. "Maybe you will return for another lesson?"

"Well," I hedged. "I loved the class...don't get me wrong...but the 'authentic' me is saying 'one dance class feels just right.'"

"Touché, Lynda—well played!"

Chapter Nine

Winning People Over with Charisma

Michael (Mike) Packman

I couldn't believe it. After all of those years of planning, scratching, clawing, and rainmaking—not to mention battling my fears—I had achieved a personal accomplishment: I had been invited to speak in front of my first major audience.

Okay, maybe it wasn't so major. It was the local chamber of commerce and a good showing at best would be a couple dozen people. Nevertheless, I could feel that combination of elation and butterflies (more like wasps) swarming in the pit of my stomach.

Am I going to freeze? Will I stutter? Will they think I'm a dope and that I don't know what I'm talking about? Or, will they be bored to tears and stay awake only by virtue of being disturbed by each other's snoring?

I went straight to work, figuring my best strategy was to concentrate on writing out my presentation. I was amazed to discover that the words flowed right out of me—probably from so many years of having envisioned myself being in this moment—and fell into a groove. Before I knew it, my motivational speech was completely typed out. I read it over a few times, rewrote it, printed it out, and then went through the hard copy the next day. Aside from minor tweaks, it was the perfect length, nailed all of my messages, and was ready to go. Best of all, it was 100% *me*.

I read several books on how to make a good presentation and, of course, had attended presentations by many elite motivational speakers, such as Dr. Greg Reid, Sharon Lechter, and Les Brown. I assumed it would all flow naturally. But, from the second I stood up, pictured myself at the podium, and began reciting my speech, I felt like a rank amateur.

Why would anyone care what I have to say? I'm coming across as totally flat. Dullsville.

I tried to take breaks from the speech to get my mind off it. I focused on other things—answering emails, checking in with clients, performing household chores, drinking hot chocolate—but nothing seemed to work. Each time I restarted my speech I felt awkward...unbalanced...*afraid*. My hands trembled. My heart thumped like a twitchy jazz drummer performing a solo. Pins and needles filled my head.

I am going to completely screw this up and make a fool of myself.

It dawned on me: I was overcome by stage fright.

What am I going to do? Oh no, I think I'm hyperventilating.

Wheatie came rushing over with a paper bag, placing it to my mouth. "Breathe in, breathe out...nice slow deep breaths....."

I followed his instructions, inhaling and exhaling into the bag. I watched it inflate and deflate. My breathing gradually returned to normal.

"Feeling better?," he asked.

I removed the bag from my face. "Yes...thank you," I said with tears wallowing in my eyes.

My husband took notice of my emotional state and hugged me.

"I don't know what I'm going to do," I blubbered. "I can't go through with this. The event is only two days away, and I'm a mess. I'll have to call them and cancel."

He looked into my eyes and insisted, "No, you won't. You can do this. I know you can. I believe in you."

"Wheatie—you're so sweet," I said. "I think you see me

through rose-colored glasses, though."

"Maybe," he smiled. "But as soon as you stand up there, everyone in the room will love you. Trust me."

"I wish I could be as confident as you."

"I have an idea. Why don't you call your friend, Pati? Maybe she'll know how to help you."

"Good idea," I considered.

Pati Maez was a friend, colleague, and spiritual leader. If anyone could get me through this, she could. I called her number right away. During our conversation, she recommended I try a meditation class nearby. I had never done anything like this before, but I figured it couldn't have been more intimidating than standing on Sohaila Handelsman's dance floor, as I had done a few weeks earlier.

An hour or so later, I found myself sitting cross-legged on a floor in a circle with a dozen other people. The lights were off, and I was trying to picture a calm stream in my head. The prompt had called for me to visualize myself as a leaf descending in the wind and landing gently in the water. A light ripple would lead me further down the stream....

"No!" I shouted, my eyes snapping open.

"What is it? Are you okay?," a soft male voice asked.

"I...I was floating peacefully along the stream...then I remembered I had to make a big speech. The stream suddenly became a gigantic waterfall, and I went crashing down—headfirst! Goodness—now I'm a failure at this, too!"

"It's all right," the man soothed me. "I presume this is your first time in a meditation class."

"Oh, how can you tell?" I joked.

"The first time is sometimes a bit awkward for newcomers," he whispered. "It's perfectly normal. One of the most difficult things is to clear your mind."

"Especially mine."

"I'm Mike. Mike Packman," the man introduced.

"Lynda Sunshine West," I said, turning to face the stranger. He was surprisingly handsome for a random person at a meditation class, with light features and close-cropped orange hair parted in the middle. He wore a comfy-looking blue shirt with loose-fitting jeans and seemed 100% calm, cool, and collected. I couldn't help but envy his state of natural, peaceful confidence.

"Listen," he said. "Maybe we should take this outside—I don't want us to disturb the others. I promise, I'm harmless. I only want to help you."

I wondered if I should have been suspicious of this total male stranger, but there was something implicitly trustworthy about him and, clearly, I hadn't been getting anywhere in this meditation class.

"Okay," I muttered as he helped me to my feet.

Once we entered the hallway and the door closed behind us, we exchanged basic information about who we are and what we do. After my turn, he told me he was the founder of Keystone National Properties. He had begun his career more than twenty years ago in finance but has been focusing mostly on real estate for many years now.

"How did you get into meditation?" I asked.

Realizing I might have sounded a bit more skeptical than I'd intended, I added: "Not that a financial person couldn't be involved in something spiritual...."

"It is a bit unusual," he said, not seeming to have taken any offense. "I've had people tell me that I help provide exactly what's needed. If there are two industries that could really benefit from meditation and the type of thinking that comes along with it, it's finance and real estate.

"I don't really have a lot of hobbies, but I make the time to meditate an hour or more pretty much every day. I've spent some time in India, studied the teachings of the great masters—including Paramahansa Yogananda, who wrote the famous book *Autobiography of a Yogi*—and have come to realize that our true happiness comes from within.

"My whole perspective on life has changed from meditating. I've become so much calmer. I own a couple of businesses and have two little kids, so you can imagine I have to fend off a lot of stress. Meditating helps me to personally deal with all of it…. Well, enough about me—tell me, Lynda, what is stressing you out so much?"

"I don't even know how to say it. I'm too embarrassed," I hedged.

"Go ahead, it's all right," he encouraged.

"Well…I'm finding success with my business, which is starting to gain some momentum. And now, since I've reached the next level, I'm expected to give my first motivational speech. At first, I really wanted to do it—like it's something I should be doing—but now I don't think I have what it takes to win over a crowd. I feel like there is an expectation of me, given what I've accomplished so far. If I bomb, I'm certain it'll be like I'm tumbling down a mountain and will lose all of my credibility. In other words, I'm scared to death of making a fool of myself."

"What frightens you most about it?," he asked.

"The whole thing!" I laughed. "When I boil it down, I guess it's that I doubt I've got what it takes to be a performer. It comes so naturally to some people, but not to me. I just don't have a magnetic personality or any charisma."

"Why would you assume you don't?," he asked. "You managed to catch my attention without even trying."

"Oh, come on," I disagreed. "You're just trying to make me feel better. You feel sorry for me."

"Nonsense," he dismissed.

99

"Let's tackle this a different way. Do you think that I have charisma?"

"Yes. Absolutely."

"And how did you get that impression? What about me makes you believe that I have charisma?"

"I don't know," I struggled. "Intangible things—like how calm you are, how you hold yourself...your confidence. I can tell that people stop and pay attention when you enter a room."

"As it happens, I do quite a bit of public speaking and have made several media appearances," he informed me. "I'll let you in on a little secret: I actually enjoy it."

Who enjoys public speaking? I'd rather stick a red-hot poker in my eye.

"You do?"

"Yes," he answered. "I'll let you in on another little secret: Anyone can be charismatic. It's a choice one makes. You already have a wonderful charismatic personality yourself, whether you realize it or not."

"No, I don't," I fired back. "I'm a mess."

"Aha! You're nervous...but that doesn't mean you aren't charismatic. Many of the world's most famous performers have suffered from serious stage fright at one time or another: Jerry Seinfeld, Barbra Streisand, Taylor Swift, Cher, Katy Perry...even the great actor, Laurence Olivier! That's not bad company to be in."

"Let's not start putting me in that category just yet," I challenged him. "You haven't answered me on how I'm charismatic."

"First of all: Like me, you are always smiling. Even when you are nervous and upset, I can see that winning smile breaking through. It's something natural, and it just helps in terms of interacting with people. You had the confidence to speak with me—a total stranger—so, whether you realize it or not, you are also very much a social person. When you smile and engage people, you are already making a connection. What you put out there is always what you get back."

"Yes," I concurred. "The law of attraction. I learned that lesson…and believe in it. It was really helpful in the beginning when I started to figure out how to get up my hill in the first place. I didn't see it connecting to public speaking, though."

"Being charismatic is about taking charge of all of the positive energy you have already inside you and projecting it out to others. Once you do that, all of those vibes will come right back to you."

Being charismatic is about taking charge of all of the positive energy you have already inside you and projecting it out to others. Once you do that, all of those vibes will come right back to you.
—Mike Packman

"I think I'm starting to get it," I absorbed. "But how do I calm down my fear of screwing up?"

"You have a lot of passion for what you do, right?"

"Certainly."

"Of course, you do," he nodded. "I could tell from the tenor of your voice when you described your business. If you were to channel your passion and excitement for your business and pretend you are speaking to just one single person in the audience—you can even gaze directly at someone you know is supportive—you have changed the dynamic. All of a sudden, instead of being on stage in front of a whole group of strange people, it's like you are having a one-on-one conversation with a friend. Audience members will pick up on your smile and your passion. They will be on your side right away because you are connecting your energy with theirs."

"What if I screw up...you know, botch what I'm saying?"

"First of all, I seriously doubt that will happen," he snapped. "Secondly, you have to remember that the audience doesn't know your speech word-for-word. How would they know if you mess up, unless you tell them or give yourself away? Just smile, tap back into your inner passion, and skip ahead to a place in your speech where you are most comfortable. You can even repeat a few words until you get back on track. You'll reclaim your groove in no time. Either way, since you have charisma, the audience is already with you. If they know you've slipped up once or twice, so what? They are already on your side. They will easily forgive a slip or two.

"In any given performance—whether someone is singing, acting, performing standup comedy, or making a business speech—audience members are paying attention to just a few things about the performer: Is she enjoying herself? Does she seem to truly want to be with them and on stage? Does she have passion for what she is talking about?

"These things are conveyed through smiling and by direct eye contact. You ever notice how some actors and performers just have charisma by standing there and not saying a word? The most charismatic people of all time—The Beatles, Clint Eastwood, Elvis Presley, Madonna, Robin Williams, Muhammad Ali, Oprah Winfrey, Marlon Brando—could just stand on stage and capture an audience's attention by doing absolutely nothing. All they did was project their inner emotions outward.

"After any performance, an audience is left with an impression. If a person comes away remembering maybe three things the person on stage or screen said, did, or sang well, it's a success. In fact, in any old classic Clint Eastwood, Arnold Schwarzenegger, or Marlon Brando movie, maybe you remember two or three lines the actor said. But that is more than enough. All you need to do is say a few words and you know exactly what movies the famous catch phrases came from: 'Go ahead, make my day'…'I'll be back'… 'Stella!'"

Naturally, I identified his imitation of each actor and chuckled with recognition.

He continued, "Select three memorable things you want your audience to remember from your presentation and really drive those home with energy, enthusiasm, and passion. The audience will pick up on them, see you shine, and even repeat them back to you later on."

"I can do that. It now sounds so clear and simple," I realized.

"That's because it all comes from within you," he explained. "How could you not love what is coming from inside you? It's the energy behind the emotions that enables us to project charisma. When we're passionate about what we're talking about, we forget about our fear and people want to listen and hear what we have to say."

It's the energy behind the emotions that enables us to project charisma. When we're passionate about what we're talking about, we forget about our fear and people want to listen and hear what we have to say.
—Mike Packman

"For example, I've never taught meditation. I'm not a teacher of any kind, much less a spiritual teacher, yet on multiple occasions people have told me that it's my true calling, and eventually maybe it will be. I'm a businessman, but it intuitively comes through how important I know this mindset is for the world. Even when I'm just casually having a conversation with one person, the next thing I know, I will be talking to a group of people. I will get questions and comments like: 'Can you teach me how to meditate?' or 'I would love to learn how to be more calm, focused, and cut out some of the chatter in my mind.' I've even been asked to lead meditations to kick off business events. This all stems from how passionate I am for this path that automatically draws positive energy to me when I speak about it."

"Which reminds me, Mike," I said. "We've talked so much that we've missed out on most of the meditation class. I'm so sorry about that."

"Don't worry about it," he smiled. "Meditation is not just about sitting with your eyes closed. It's how you channel those experiences and apply them in your interactions with others. Selfless service is one of the key components, so allowing me to help you has been your gift to me."

"Maybe you can do me one more favor then…."

"What is it? Name it."

"Can you teach me how to meditate?"

"You bet! Let's get started."

Chapter Ten

Cooperating and Collaborating—Not Competing

Dennis Haber

At long last, I was discovering firsthand the real power of momentum in business. I was rolling forward in continuous motion and had several successes under my belt. All of my clients seemed to be reaping the rewards of my training, and I felt that I was making a powerful impact on their lives. Several of my clients had overcome their fear—much as I had accomplished for myself—and were already becoming established public speakers in their own right. On top of that, the coaching side of my business was exploding thanks to word-of-mouth recommendations. I was making money hand-over-fist and showing real profit.

Buried deep in the back of my mind, I was waiting for the "other shoe" to drop. Something was going to block my descent down the mountain, causing me to stumble and fall. I had no idea when or what it was going to be—or how hard I would feel the direct impact—until…it happened. It felt like the entire weight of my body had smacked into a tree at one hundred miles per hour.

Without getting into too many specifics, let's just say that Morganna—someone I knew and trusted—was copying my business model and mastermind concept. I was even getting wind that she was approaching my clients for business.

How dare she! I'd confided everything in Morganna and

105

shared all of my business strategies. Now she has the audacity to steal my idea and clients?

I never experienced betrayal like this before. In fact, I hadn't even encountered much in the way of direct competition. My head filled with renewed doubt about what I was doing and where I was headed. Could I no longer trust anyone? Was I able to compete head-to-head against someone else?

Wheatie felt I was on the verge of imploding and urged me to get out of the house right away. "Go to the gym, go for a run...*anything*! You have to let out some steam. Then you can calm down and think about this objectively."

"You're right. Thanks, Wheatie," I said. "Good advice."

I carelessly flung my pants and blouse across the bedroom and tugged on my favorite workout pants, a tank top, and my lucky Leukemia & Lymphoma Society ball cap. I rushed down the steps with my phone, keys, and wallet and grabbed a bottle of water from the fridge before heading outside to my car.

My thoughts became so foggy and filled with rage that I sleepwalked the drive to the gym. I somehow made it onto an available treadmill and didn't give a second's thought to stretching or warming up as my finger tapped the accelerator button...

Faster, faster, faster...

My heartbeat throbbed and my chest wheezed, but I didn't care. Something urged me to continue at an increasingly frenetic pace.

Morganna. How can she do this to me? I don't want to wish evil upon anyone, but I wouldn't be too upset if she happened to suffer from some non-fatal malady—like incontinence or chronic flatulence.

My phone had been turned up all the way, so when my ringtone blasted Pat Benatar's "You Better Run," I was nearly jolted off the treadmill.

No. Don't look. Don't answer. You must resist at all costs. It's only going to make you angrier and more frustrated. Exercise is your time...work can't interfere with it. This call could be even worse business news, which is something I don't need right now.

But...what if Wheatie is trying to contact me? Or, if one of my clients has something urgent to discuss? Or, it's a new potential client? I have to be there and available for my people when they need me. If not, maybe they'll go to someone else like Morganna for help.

I'll just peek at who it is. Maybe it's a telemarketer and I can ignore it. What harm could it cause?

Both arguments closed in on me as the phone rang and buzzed full force a second and third time. Soon it would be too late, and I'd miss it.

Temptation proved too great, and I picked up the phone to check caller i.d. It was Roxanne, one of my newest clients. She and I were only just getting started working together. She seemed really smart and sweet, and I doubted anything she might say to me would make me more upset than I was at that moment.

"Hi Roxanne, how are you?" I asked, hoping she wouldn't notice my huffing and puffing.

I might have been imagining things, but something in her voice sounded different. Distant, perhaps. "I'm fine, Lynda," she replied. "Is now a good time to talk?"

"Sure," I lied, grabbing the handle of the treadmill with my free hand for support as I continued my run. "What's up?"

"I wanted to tell you in person rather than text or email. I have something difficult to say to you," she hedged.

"Go ahead," I said. "You can trust me."

"I know I can," she said. "It's just that...."

My head began to swirl. I could feel the sweat pouring down my eyes and cheeks.

MOMENTUM

Thank heaven this isn't a Zoom call. What could be so difficult for her to say?

"You know I think the world of you, Lynda. You're so *real* and gracious. I really like you a lot...."

Now this was getting serious. "Roxanne, just give it to me straight. What's wrong? I can hear it in your voice."

"It's nothing personal...nothing you've done or haven't done. I think you are really great."

Uh-oh. Why is this sounding like a breakup?

"Okay," I steeled myself.

"Well, frankly, I was approached by another coach. Someone who also happens to do training for live videos and runs a mastermind," she informed me. "I'm so sorry, but I decided to go with her. Again, it's not you at all. It's just that...I don't know, she and I just clicked. If I could have two coaches, I would continue with you...but I just don't have the money or the time...."

Her voice trailed off into gibberish.

Kabam! I'm losing a client to a competitor. This has never happened to me before. Will others follow suit?

I felt dazed and wounded. My head and body pounded from the impact of the deathblow. I had no idea what I was saying, but I vaguely imagined it was something like: "I'm so sorry you feel that way. Is there anything else I can do?"

All of a sudden, I felt as if I was losing consciousness—like I was going to pass out. I began to teeter and tilt off the treadmill. I became somewhat aware of the phone twirling out of my hand while the other one lost its grip on the handle. The rotations of the treadmill were too great, and my legs couldn't retain their footing. I tripped and wobbled, flopping dangerously across the machine.

I was headed for a major tumble when someone grabbed hold of me and steadied me in place. I watched in slow motion as an arm reached over to hit the emergency stop button on my treadmill. The person held me firmly in place until the machine's rumblings stuttered and ceased.

I leaned into the kind person for support while I caught my breath. "Are you all right?" a male voice asked. "Here—drink some water."

The man handed me my open water bottle and brought it to my mouth. I was able to mutter "Thank you" before placing the bottle between my lips and gulping down the cool liquid.

"Easy," the man said. "Would you like me to get some help?"

I emphatically nodded "No" with my hand raised. My breathing returned to normal, and my mind began to get back into focus. "Thank you. I'm already feeling a lot better. I can stand on my own."

He released me. I balanced myself on my treadmill and toweled off my forehead and face.

"You nearly wiped out," the man observed.

I was finally able to get a good look at the dignified, sixty-something gentleman with brown hair who had saved me from injury. He struck me as being pretty athletic as he hopped off his treadmill and made his way toward a Wet Wipe™ dispenser. He bent down underneath the dispenser, retrieved my cell phone, and looked it over while heading back toward me. "Looks like it didn't get damaged," he said, returning the device to me.

"Thank you so much," I said, also inspecting the phone. "I really appreciate your help."

"That must have been some phone call," the man reflected.

"Yes, it was," I admitted.

"Do you care to talk about it?" he offered. "I don't mean to pry but, as it happens, I'm a PPS."

"A PPS? What's that?"

"A Professional Problem-Solver. In layperson's terms, I coach people in their business, personal, and family lives. I help people conquer fear and self-doubt, so they can figure out their next moves and excel. Maybe I can help you—or just listen?"

He extended his hand to me. I didn't hesitate to shake.

"Dennis Haber."

"Lynda Sunshine West," I chuckled, revealing some embarrassment as I next uttered: "I also happen to coach people."

"What a small world!" he shouted. "Listen, setbacks happen to the best of us. The important thing is to get back on track as soon as possible. When the mind is not cooperating and collaborating with the *self*, you end up criticizing yourself and others and miss so many opportunities."

"You're absolutely right, Dennis, it's just…you know, so frustrating. Everything was going really well for me. My business was gaining amazing momentum—and then the other shoe dropped. A woman I know copied my entire business model. I'm pretty sure she's poached one of my clients."

"I can see how that would be upsetting," Dennis commented. "But there is a positive side to competition."

A positive side to competition? Is this guy for real?

"You seem skeptical," he grinned. "I understand. Like most people, you are looking at what this person did as only a negative. I'll give you a counter-perspective. First of all, there is the flattering aspect to it. Obviously, your business model has a great deal of merit, and this other person admired what you were doing enough to copy it."

This made a little bit of sense. "Go on," I encouraged.

"Another positive side of competition happens when you compare the rate of progress of your own personal improvement. When you compete with yourself, it is the healthiest form of competition. The singular significant goal in life is to just become better. Before anything else, being ready for success requires that you have a positive conversation with yourself. And, since we have conversations with ourselves more than anyone else, this dialogue is very determinative," he explained.

Another positive side of competition happens when you compare the rate of progress of your own personal improvement. When you compete with yourself, it is the healthiest form of competition. The singular significant goal in life is to just become better. Before anything else, being ready for success requires that you have a positive conversation with yourself.
—Dennis Haber

"So, you are suggesting I talk to myself more?" I laughed.

"Yes, exactly!" Dennis reacted, sipping from his own water bottle. "And you have to listen to what you have to say. Your inner voice must be your greatest cheerleader."

"Rah-rah-rah!" I gestured as if I were holding invisible pom-poms and with a sense of disbelief. "But that doesn't help me swat away this competitor."

"The way to meet a competitive threat is to have already done the hard work. A company doesn't *handle* a competitive threat; it *prepares* for a competitive threat. After all, once the ship has capsized, it's too late for precaution. You lost one client— okay, it hurts, but you accept it and move on and prepare better. The questions to ask yourself are: *What am I doing to maintain my current client relationships? How am I keeping them happy? What am I doing to stay ahead of threats?* There will always be competition in your crosshairs, but you have to stay one step ahead of them at all times."

"That's really good advice," I considered. "I guess I've been so focused on moving forward that I haven't been paying enough attention to who might be coming at me from behind. I should be preparing myself to stick my leg out to trip competitors."

"I wouldn't go that far," Dennis considered. "I think it's smart for you to toughen up in business. Mental toughness is critical. It enhances clarity of thought and provides the strength to bulldoze through obstacles. But there is no need to play dirty, and I doubt you're the type anyway. Business professionals who cooperate and collaborate with *themselves* end up being the ones who find true success and defeat the competition."

"Okay...."

"I can see you're puzzled, Lynda. Let me unpack that for you. When you collaborate and cooperate with your *self*—and I mean to stress that as two words by intent—you give yourself an opportunity to create a better version of *yourself*. Turning your worries about competitive threats inward is a mind shift of exponential proportion because it destroys negative self-talk. This leads to mental toughness.

"In your case, the client who went with someone else doesn't matter. You probably had nothing whatsoever to do with her decision. It's just a matter of fit for her. It happens. But if I were you, once you've had a chance to shower and clear your head, you should call the client and wish her the best. You never know when she'll come back to you or recommend someone else for your business.

"As for your competitor: The next time you see her, congratulate her on her business. See if there is any advantage to partnering with her."

Partner? With that b-i-t-c-h? Never!

"All right, I can tell by your expression that the wound is still too fresh. Over time, however, you may find that her motives were not as evil as you originally perceived them to be and you can find ways to collaborate. If not, it doesn't matter. You will be improving to become a better version of yourself, which, from my standpoint, is already pretty impressive. I want you to remember what a professor once said to me: 'Good, better, best. Never let it rest. Till your good is better and your better is best.' Constant improvement should be the only goal."

I want you to remember what a professor once said to me: 'Good, better, best. Never let it rest. Till your good is better and your better is best.' Constant improvement should be the only goal.
—Dennis Haber

"I love that," I gushed. "Maybe I should be paying *you* as *my* coach."

"Nah," he dismissed. "I can tell you are like me. We both truly enjoy helping people. That's more than enough compensation."

"You know," I proposed, "I just got a second wind. You up for a run?"

"Are you sure?" he asked. "You nearly passed out a few minutes ago."

"I'm good. Fully rested and hydrated," I stated.

"Okay," he accepted. "Just take it easy this time."

"You bet."

We went on our respective machines and started up our treadmills. I could tell by his pace, posture, and breathing that he was an experienced runner and in excellent shape. I didn't make the mistake of trying to keep up with him—at least at first: I began with a brisk walk and built up to a jog, which I easily maintained.

"Doing all right over there?" he checked in.

"Yup," I replied. "Just great. But you'll have to tell me: What's your story? How did you get to be so mentally tough

113

and turn out to be such a good coach?"

"Well," he began. "We have some time to kill and calories to burn, so I'm happy to tell you about it. My childhood dream was to become a doctor—a heart surgeon. I loved that special feeling of helping people. Whenever I went to a doctor's office with my Mom, I imagined how good it must be to help others. When she went to the butcher, she would bring home various organs: hearts, livers, and spleens. I would dissect them."

"Yuck!" I exclaimed. "I mean...cool!"

He laughed before continuing: "When I was thirteen, my parents bought me *Gray's Anatomy*, the book every doctor in America has on his or her bookshelf. I remember memorizing paragraphs and pretending I was a doctor. I regurgitated paragraphs of medical information back to anyone who would listen.

"But I ended up going on a different path and didn't attend medical school. I learned that you can never reach a dream if you take your eyes off the prize and focus on the obstacles instead. Organic chemistry did me in. At that point, I had not yet developed the mental toughness to keep the doctor dream alive.

"I went to law school instead. In my second year, temporary paralysis and brain surgery turned my life upside down. It was a long climb back to normalcy. Since everything exists in potential, it was all up to me to decide and determine the kind of life I was going to have. Two things had to happen. I needed to: 1) see the possibility of a better future; and 2) realize I could help make it a reality. These are critical lessons to learn. Magic happens when you develop the skill sets to match your desires. For a twenty-four-year-old, life is supposed to be easy. I learned the first law of life at that time: The sooner you learn that life is not easy, or fair, the better off you will be."

"Hold on a second," I processed. "A moment ago...did you

say you had 'brain surgery'?"

He nodded and revealed, "I suppose I've had my share of health scares. After my experience with brain surgery, I thought I was in the clear and impervious to anything happening to me again. But then I was thrown for a loop when I was diagnosed with stage four cancer. Thankfully, I have been in the clear for four years. Except now I have a pesky knee problem and need surgery for that…which is why I'm taking such good care of my body to help with the recovery."

"That is so impressive, Dennis," I raved. "But I don't follow something. You just said you became a lawyer instead of a doctor. I thought you're a Professional Problem-Solver?"

"I am," he answered. "I always gravitated to the motivation/ self-help arena. After the cancer and retiring, I wondered what I would do with the rest of my life. I knew I was someone who enjoyed helping people solve their problems and looked for something to do along those lines. I even searched online for ideas. I discovered I could become a certified Ziglar Trainer and Coach. After all, I had so many of Zig Ziglar's books and tapes. I've even written my first self-improvement book, *Don't Play With Fire: How To Keep Your Greatness From Going Up In Flames*. Take one guess who contributed the foreword?"

"It can't be Zig Ziglar—he passed away a while ago."

"Close! His son, Tom. His sisters, Julie and Cindy, provided testimonials for the book as well."

"Amazing," I complimented him. "Despite all of the obstacles you've faced, you've become incredibly successful."

"Success is not necessarily what you've done with your life, but what you *could have done*. I'm still working on the *could have done* part."

"What a great way to look at it, Dennis," I said. "Imagine my good fortune in happening to stumble on the treadmill right next to you!"

"Right back at you, Lynda," he winked, slowing down his treadmill to catch his breath and checking out my dashboard. "I'm in awe. Not only were you able to get right back on that treadmill after nearly collapsing, somehow you've already burned just as many calories as I have and are still going!"

"Well, what do you know—you're right!" I beamed. "Thanks to you, I feel great again. My inner voice is telling me I'm back on track and will regain my business momentum in no time. I'm going to focus on improving my *self*, leaving my competition stranded on the bunny slope!"

Part Four

Final Finish

Wise Man #4 - Brian Smith

Many entrepreneurs believe that success is far down the road. I don't see it that way. I think you have to celebrate each mini-success you accomplish while you're putting the production together. This will help you build enough motivation to cross the finish line.

As your business expands, you'll need to recruit a team to help you get the work done and scale up. However, you must develop a great deal of courage and confidence *before* you can lead other people. If you think you'll be able to develop those traits once people are hired, you're doing it backwards.

When I started UGG, it felt like I was pulling out my own fingernails every day. I was a typical entrepreneur. I did everything myself and wore all of the hats. I thought that no one could do anything as well as I could. Delegation was extremely difficult for me, which seems to be the case for most entrepreneurs.

You have to ask yourself: "If an employee only does something 80% of the way I want it, can I live with that?" Once you arrive at that conclusion, it's amazing how easy it becomes to trust people and delegate. The best leaders are able to have faith, let go, and praise people when they come through for you.

After you've climbed up and down your mountain, it's important to move on to the next thing. When I sold UGG, I patented a new type of pre-cast wall panel that incorporates lightweight concrete and steel studs. At the time, it was a breakthrough technology and over one hundred structures were built. Then the 2008 recession hit. We went through a three-year halt in construction, which set into play the events that would lead to the eventual demise of the company.

No one is immune to failure and tumbling down the mountain. It can happen at any time to the best of us. Sometimes it's self-inflicted; other times it's beyond our control. When that happens, you have to pick yourself up, learn from your mistakes, let go of any self-blame, and head right back up a new mountain. You will come out the other side wiser, stronger, and more successful. As Napoleon Hill wrote in his book *Outwitting the Devil*: "Experiences of adversity were among the most fortunate and profitable of all my experiences."

After my pre-cast wall panel business shuttered, I went down an entirely different path and wrote *The Birth of a Brand*, which is like a roadmap for entrepreneurs. That led me to try public speaking.

During my downtime, I climbed a real mountain—Mount Kilimanjaro. It was a phenomenal experience, although I admit I hated it the whole time I was up there. I couldn't wait to come down. I'm not anemic, but I don't have a normal amount of red cells. I really suffered on top of that mountain. But I made it without having to take any oxygen or drugs.

My main point is that, when one opportunity had reached its natural conclusion or crumbled, I already had my eye on my next major challenge. And, no matter what I ended up doing, I made sure I would forget about any past failures and find a way to be *the best* at my new undertaking. If you can become the best at something, you cannot help but become successful.

This doesn't necessarily mean waiting for some huge payoff, like selling the company fifteen years down the road for seven figures. It means working hard and improving yourself, your products, and your business. Every day you must attempt to add at least one more brick to the wall. Once the brick has been set, celebrate your mini success before placing the next one. Before you know it, you've completed the job and you'll have a whole wall full of mini-successes to reflect back on.

The following impressive people will be cheering you on to have a successful final finish: *Elizabeth Moors*, *Kym Glass*, and *Pati Maez* as a special added bonus.

MOMENTUM

Chapter Eleven

Deciding to Be Determined, Driven— and Focused

Elizabeth Moors

During the weeks that followed, I was pleased that my concerns about competition didn't amount to much of anything. Or, at least they no longer stood as a hindrance. Dennis Haber's advice to ignore the competition, focus inward, and continue to improve myself made a world of difference.

My business resumed its course and I was regaining momentum. In fact, having some money to burn, I decided to hop on a flight with my Wheatie from San Diego to Colorado Springs, where we could hit a local casino. How I love to play the slot machines! Of course, while we "happened to be there," we were going to visit my brother, who planned to drive us to Cripple Creek, a quaint town nearby.

"Attention all passengers in Group D," a woman shouted on the loudspeaker. "Now boarding Group D...."

Wheatie tapped my knee and said, "C'mon, that's us, we gotta go."

I held up my finger to indicate "just one minute." He stood in front of me with his bags and ticket printout at the ready. Wheatie was always polite and supportive, but I could tell he was thinking I was going to be a challenge every step of the way on this trip. My phone had been *buzzing* and *dinging* with incessant calls, texts, and emails the instant we left the house. At the moment we were summoned to board, I was locked on

121

a call with a potential client: "I offer a range of services: speaker training, video training, my Women Action Takers Podcast, individual coaching…. Yes, you can mix-and-match or you can try one piece out and then add something on later…."

"Last call for Group D….."

Wheatie flapped his arms longingly toward the gate entrance. "We're not going to have any space in the overhead compartment for our bags," he implored.

I covered the phone and said, "Okay, okay. Got it."

I tucked the phone under my chin as I scavenged my purse for the printout of my ticket.

"What are you looking for?" Wheatie asked.

"My ticket," I replied. "I can't seem to find it."

"That's because I have both of them right here," Wheatie laughed, holding up what now appeared to be two ticket printouts.

"Oh yeah, I forgot I gave you mine," I muttered.

"Final call for all passengers flying to Colorado Springs…."

I fumbled to collect my suitcase, handbag, and cup of hot chocolate while continuing to remain on the phone and listen to my newest client. My overloaded handbag dropped off my shoulder to my wrist, but I caught it just in time and didn't tip my cup or lose my phone.

Wheatie came right to my aid, taking my suitcase and wheeling it along with his possessions toward the ticket counter. Somehow, he managed to balance all of these items quite well.

As for me—well, I struggled even without having to manage my rolling suitcase. I began to feel a crimp in my neck from having cradled the phone to my face in such an awkward position for so long. I scurried to catch up with Wheatie as he presented our tickets to the airline attendant and gestured that I was with him.

"You're lucky—another second and we were closing the

door," the attendant said, scanning our tickets.

I continued to listen on the phone as I made my way through the center aisle, squeezing past people of all shapes and sizes. Some were cooperative and at least made a slight effort to allow me to pass; others seemed intent on blocking me as they made sure their jackets, suitcases, and bags were 100% perfectly arranged in the overhead compartments. One large man stood in front of a seat to chat with someone and refused to budge even after I said, "Excuse me." I somehow sucked it in and burrowed past him, although I missed a few words my client said on the phone.

I recognized my row when I spotted Wheatie placing our suitcases in the overhead compartment. While continuing to juggle my phone, I tossed a couple things up there as well before he gestured for me to take my place in the middle seat.

"Yes, we can meet right when I return from my trip on Tuesday," I informed my client while settling down. "Evening would be fine at around—oh, wait, hold on. I have another call. It'll just be a sec."

I pressed a button on my phone to respond to the other caller. "Oh, hi!" I shouted. "I'm glad you caught me. I'm on the plane, just about to take off. But I thought you'd like to know that I like your ideas for my website, and I want to get started right away."

Wheatie poked me in the shoulder to indicate that the stewardess was seeking my attention. "Ma'am, please buckle your seatbelt. And place your phone on airplane mode or turn it off for takeoff."

I mouthed the words "Sure, no problem" while handing my hot chocolate cup to my husband and reaching underneath my bottom to find my seatbelt. "Can you get it done by the thirtieth? I really need it completed by the end of the month," I spouted into the phone. "Okay...uh huh...okay...."

When I finally grasped a piece of the seatbelt, I traced the material with my hand to find the metal end. I couldn't seem to figure out where it was, so I tugged hard on the material.

"Hey!" shouted the perturbed woman seated in the window seat on my left.

"Sorry," I said, now aware that she had been sitting on my strap.

"Here," she said, handing the shiny end of the strap to me. "If you weren't so distracted, maybe you would have had some manners."

"Sorry," I repeated to the woman without looking at her. I was more concerned that I couldn't get my web guy off the phone and had left my client dangling. Meanwhile, the plane was starting to move, and it was finally dawning on me that I shouldn't be on the phone at all at this point.

"Listen," I directed into the phone. "I really have to go. Send me an email with all the details. Bye."

I pressed my phone to return to my client, but either she had given up or we had been disconnected.

I can't be rude to my client like that. I'll just call her back really fast.

I tapped my client's number and listened through several ringtones.

"Ma'am," berated the stewardess. "Turn your phone off *right now!*"

"I just have to tell my client one important thing—it'll be one second, I swear."

The stewardess looked like she was going to have a hissy fit as I allowed the call to continue to ring. She hovered over me like a school marm as I heard my client's voice mail recording.

"Ma'am! We are not allowed to take off if you are using an unapproved electronic device. You'll hold up our flight and everyone on board will get pretty angry."

"I think you should listen to her," Wheatie urged me.

"Fine. I am, I am..." At last, the recording bleeped, and I blurted out: "Hi, this is Lynda calling you back...sorry we were disconnected before. I'm on a plane about to take off, so I'll call you back as soon as I land. Bye."

I hope I sounded okay...I rushed my message. But what else could I do with Hilda, the wicked stewardess of the west, sneering down at me?

"Put it in airplane mode, please," the stewardess barked. *"Now."*

"Oh yes, of course," I said, feeling like a child who was being spanked. I tapped on my phone when it rang and buzzed again. My heart did cartwheels as I looked at caller i.d.

An important potential partner! A big one. I've been waiting months for her to call me. I have to answer...I can't resist.

I tapped the phone and brought it to my ear. "Hi there, this is Lynda," I began. "I'm about to take off on a plane and am getting dirty looks from the stewardess...oh?.... Really? You want me to help you organize a networking event. Wow, I would love to—"

Before I knew what was happening, the phone was snatched right out of my hand.

I watched open-mouthed as the stewardess turned off the phone and dangled it in the air.

My potential business partner—how could the stewardess do this to me?!

"Don't worry," she said. "It will be safe. I'll return it when we are in the air and the captain says it's okay."

I was flustered and angry, but caught Wheatie's "I told you so" grin and backed down. Of course, deep down I knew the stewardess was right. The airplane's safety comes first, and I was being rude.

How did I become one of those obnoxious people I used to

frown upon?

Wheatie handed my hot chocolate cup back to me. "It's probably ice cold by now," he observed.

"I don't mind. You know I like it better a little cold," I said, taking a long gulp of the tepid liquid.

I stewed as the airplane made its way down the runway and we waited for our turn to take off. Finally, the craft jostled with increasing speed until it tipped upward and soared in the air.

I want my phone back. I know I would have to keep it in airplane mode, but I can't be without it. There are things I could still be doing with it to be productive. It's like she removed a limb. Or a major organ.

I gulped back the last drop from the cup and rummaged through my bag for my copy of *Think and Grow Rich for Women*. After alternating my gaze between the aisle—on the lookout for the stewardess returning with my phone—and flipping a few pages, I reached back into my bag to dig out my notebook and pen and jot down some business ideas.

I perked up when a deep male voice came on the loudspeaker: "This is your Captain speaking. We have reached our cruising altitude of 32,000 feet. We are seeing clear skies and expect a smooth ride. We shouldn't have any bumps along the way. You may now use your approved electronic devices at this time, but please keep them in airplane mode. You are also free to move about the cabin...."

I reached my hand up to summon the stewardess.

"What are you doing?," Wheatie asked.

"I want my phone back," I answered.

"Relax," he assured me. "You'll get it back. Don't be so impatient. A few minutes without your phone is a good thing."

"Amen," a female voice interrupted.

Who said that? Is a total stranger getting involved in my business?

I turned to the woman seated on my left, prepared to give her a piece of my mind. I hadn't noticed her until then—even when I attempted to yank the belt out from underneath her. She had shortish light brown hair and was wearing an orange v-neck. She was engrossed in a parenting magazine.

"Were you talking to me?," I asked.

Why on earth did I say that? I sound like psycho Robert De Niro in Taxi Driver.

I had been learning to be stronger, tougher, and more confident in my exchanges with people. Maybe I had gone too far and was coming on too strong?

"Yes, as a matter of fact, *I was*," she admitted, continuing to look down at her magazine.

I decided to tone it down a bit. I didn't see any need to get into a battle with a stranger during a flight—especially when both of us were captive for the duration. "I was just wondering…what you meant by saying 'amen.' Were you making some kind of statement about me?"

She sighed, placing the magazine down on her lap. "You're a business professional, right? An entrepreneur?"

"What does that have to do with—"

"Of course, you are," she surmised. "Listen, I don't want to pry…it happens I'm a certified John Maxwell coach, so I tend to notice things about businesspeople."

God, do I feel foolish. After all of the amazing people I have accidentally encountered and learned from over the past few months—Annie Evans, David Blackford, Nadia Fleury, Krysten Maracle, Paige Panzarello, Amy Burton, Mike Packman, Sohaila Handelsman, and Dennis Haber, Dr. Greg Reid, Frank Shankwitz, Brian Smith, and Ron Klein, I still haven't learned that you never know whom you might randomly meet, especially on an airplane.

I knew I had to backtrack. I hadn't anticipated that the person next to me would be someone relatable—perhaps even beneficial.

"You're a *business coach*?" I gasped. "Perhaps we got off on the wrong foot. I'm Lynda Sunshine West. Yes, I'm an entrepreneur."

"Elizabeth Moors, nice to meet you," she introduced without offering eye contact. "I actually stopped coaching—I decided it's not my forte because I'm an Aspie. I see myself as a speaker and author. At heart, I'm an entrepreneur like you."

"Forgive me for asking...*Aspie*?"

"Yes, it's sometimes what we call ourselves—people who have Asperger Syndrome, that is. My son is also an Aspie. I recognized he was on the spectrum when he was about five and then later had it confirmed at school. I was told to put him on medication and accept that he would probably not amount to much. Needless to say, I wasn't going to accept that and started doing my own program with him.

"In order for me to ensure my son would have the best possible chance of a successful and independent life, I gave up my real estate practice and we became a one income family. We lost everything and have been rebuilding since 2010. Ever since then, I've turned to speaking and writing books. My latest book is *Taking Charge of You: Raising an Independent & Successful Child with Aspergers.*"

Asperger Syndrome. Now I understand.

"Your story is fascinating, Elizabeth. I'm so impressed with your background, the book, and the fact that you have made a career out of your knowledge and expertise. But I have to ask: How did you identify me as an entrepreneur so quickly?"

"It's pretty obvious. I can tell you are an entrepreneur by your phone conversations and manner. You can't keep still or be without your device for a split-second. You flit from one shiny object to the next."

"That's true. You have me pegged," I conceded, coming to

a realization: "I suppose I have 'squirrel syndrome.' I get easily distracted. It's just that…well, everything excites me. I feel like there is so much I have to do…so much I *want* to do."

"I hope you don't mind if I give you some good hard advice," she stated.

"No, not at all," I said. "In fact, I welcome it."

"Determination can be a very good thing. It means you are resolute and have made a decision *to do* something. But it doesn't necessarily mean you're going to get it done. You also have to be driven and singularly focused on your goal. Otherwise, you won't achieve it because you are allowing obstacles and opportunities along the way to distract you. Do you have a company purpose?"

It all came back to me: my lesson learned from David Blackford.

Purpose: To help women discover their value and learn how to share their voices with the world.

"Yes," I sheepishly replied.

"Does everything you do—every single activity—funnel into your purpose?"

"Um….mostly."

"That's not good enough, Lynda," she sharply stated. "If you really want your business to continue to gain momentum, you must be driven, determined—and focused. Being determined involves doing what is necessary to be successful, even if it involves taking risks or going against the norm. Being driven is when all of your behaviors and actions are aimed at achieving success. Being focused means intensely sticking to your purpose, business model, and goals—and putting aside everything else. If you are not determined, driven, and focused, you won't have continued business momentum. You could have a wonderful product or service, but if you are unwilling to do whatever is necessary to make it a success and avoid distractions, then you'll never achieve your desired end result."

Have I told her about my quest to gain momentum for my business? I don't think so...how did she happen to know all of this? Incredible!

Being determined involves doing what is necessary to be successful, even if it involves taking risks or going against the norm. Being driven is when all of your behaviors and actions are aimed at achieving success. Being focused means intensely sticking to your purpose, business model, and goals—and putting aside everything else. If you are not determined, driven, and focused, you won't have any business momentum. You could have a wonderful product or service, but if you are unwilling to do whatever is necessary to make it a success and avoid distractions, then you'll never achieve your desired end result."
—Elizabeth Moors

"I love that," I said. "Please, Elizabeth, tell me more about how to avoid distractions. I could really use the extra advice. I guess I didn't realize how bad things were getting for me. I was too busy enjoying the momentum of being involved with so many people and projects. Like I said, it was kind of thrilling."

"That's just it," Elizabeth reflected. "It *is* exciting. There is great temptation to working with each and every person. But you have to distinguish between what fits in with your purpose and goals and which ones you can discard. Sometimes it can be difficult to choose and let go, especially when it comes to people who seem so anxious to work with you and vice versa.

The problem is, the more momentum you build, the bigger your business becomes—and then you have to shave off some things to keep your priorities in check and continue to get things done well."

"I also don't want to turn my back on people. I may need to go back to them later on," I pointed out.

"Right. Good point. The first thing to do is discard the people who don't share your business vision, don't support you, take up too much of your time, and don't add to your bottom line," she instructed.

"How do I accomplish that without being rude?"

"You might say something like 'I really appreciate what you do and would love to work with you, but right now I have other business priorities to focus on.' It's perfectly okay to say, 'No.' I'm sure they hear it all the time."

"How ironic. I've come a long way. I used to be one of those people who constantly heard 'No,'" I chuckled. "What do I do if the distractions happen to be non-business related? I mean, friends and family who chew up my time. Of course, I'm not referring to my husband, Wheatie...."

I gestured to him on my right, and he responded by politely saying "Hi" to Elizabeth. She waved back in acknowledgement.

"You have to establish internal rules for working hours and then stick to them. Just because you are home and your own boss doesn't mean you aren't working. Sometimes people— especially loved ones—don't understand that. They think: 'Oh, she's home and answered the phone, so we can talk forever.' As an entrepreneur, your time is far too precious. Every day, from the moment you wake up, you have to carve out your working hours. Block them off on your calendar, if you must— even if you don't have specific appointments."

"What do I say when people I care about want to talk during my busy work hours?"

"Something along the lines of 'I really want to chat with you—but I have a lot of work to do today. Can I call you back tonight?'"

"Family and friends can get pretty persistent," I inserted. "They'll say, 'Oh, I just have one thing to tell you, it'll only take five minutes.' I get drawn in. An hour later, we're still on the phone."

"I hear you. I get that all the time, too," Elizabeth commiserated. "If it's truly important, then of course you'd have to stay on the line. Loved ones come first. If the person says, 'It'll only take five minutes,' tell her 'I'll give you *ten*.' But then you have to be tough and watch the clock. After ten minutes, you must stick to your guns and say, 'I'm sorry but, like I said, I only had ten minutes. I really do want to finish the conversation. Can I call you back tonight and we'll continue where we left off?'"

"I guess I've toughened up in some areas, but not enough in terms of guarding my time," I realized.

"Exactly," Elizabeth said. "I'm not a people pleaser like you seem to be—but I never want to hurt someone's feelings, either. I've learned how to be respectful while at the same time demanding that other people respect my time. Think of it this way: Money can sometimes be replaced, but time cannot."

"You are awesome, Elizabeth," I gushed. "Would you mind if I pick your brain for the rest of the flight? Who knows what other wisdom you have to impart to me. Ooh…I have a podcast called Women Action Takers Podcast and am always looking for amazing guests to interview. You have so much value to offer my audience. If you're interested, let's talk about it toward the end of the flight."

"I'm in. After all, I'm also an Action Taker," Elizabeth beamed.

Money can sometimes be replaced, but time cannot.
—Elizabeth Moors

"Ma'am?" a familiar voice called to me.

I shifted to my right and saw the stewardess reaching her hand toward me to return my phone. "Here. You can have this back. I'm sorry I had to take it from you, but airline rules are pretty strict, and you didn't seem to be listening."

"No, *I'm* the one who should apologize," I said. "I was on the phone too long. It was selfish of me. I could have held up the flight and all of these passengers. I'm really sorry."

"Well, it's okay now," she softened. "You can turn it on, but please leave it on airplane mode."

"You know what?" I asked, glancing over at Elizabeth. "I don't trust myself. Can you hold on to it for the rest of the flight? I need to detox a bit and talk to my new friend here."

The stewardess raised one eyebrow and said, "Okay…if that's what you really want," before heading further down the aisle.

Two hands patted my shoulders, one from each respective side: Wheatie and Elizabeth.

Ah, I must have done something right. I have learned to "Just say no to being a squirrel."

MOMENTUM

Chapter Twelve

Leading Others with Courage to Fearless Freedom

Kym Glass

The finish line at the end of the mountain was directly in front of me. I had gained enough momentum to trek up the mountain and slide back down at a brisk pace without crashing and falling flat on my face. Elizabeth Moors had prevented me from becoming my own worst enemy when it came to my finding balance between working smart vs. working hard and over-extending myself.

Was there anything left for me to learn? You bet! I used to be that cocky type of person who thought I knew everything but, since I started this journey, have learned that I could never be doing everything 100% right all the time. Most entrepreneurs—even the super successful—recognize that there are always tweaks and improvements to be made and people who know things that you don't.

Well, I reasoned, there was no sense in waiting around for my next challenge—or second mountain to climb—before finally celebrating my accomplishments. The timing for a mini-vacation seemed just right because I was experiencing a mini-summer lull before things were going to ramp up again in the Fall. I was overdue for a recharge.

I had a lot to look forward to; my business was expanding with such fervor I realized I was going to have to hire at least a couple of people in order to manage the workload. I was thrilled at the possibility of being able to pass along all of my lessons to other people who had big career ambitions.

With that in mind, Wheatie and I hopped on a plane to the home of Elvis impersonators, inexpensive buffets, amazing household-name live acts, fantastic shows, and endless rows of slot machines: *Woot woot*!

We lit up with excitement as the taxi pulled up in front of the extraordinary Treasure Island Hotel in Las Vegas. It was night-time and the proscenium-shaped building was lit up in glowing, streaking colors. As fortune would have it (pun intended), we arrived just in time for the famous pirate battle scene: the orchestral music blasted in our ears as the pirate ship buoyed across the water and the actors played their parts with gusto, shouting out orders and swooping down from ropes. The British commander stood firm as cannons roared, smoke blared, men screamed in anguish, and bodies and barrels tumbled and flew across the ship. All of this Disney-like excitement—and we hadn't even checked in yet!

When the show ended, we plowed through the crowd and through the hotel's revolving glass doors. We stepped toward reception, where Wheatie took care of all the details: handing his credit card, signing papers, receiving our room keys, asking about the gym location, hearing about breakfast hours, and so on. Meanwhile, I soaked everything in.

Once we were settled at the front desk, we wheeled our luggage toward the elevator and stepped inside, where two beautiful, polished businesswomen were in mid-conversation. "I can't wait until tomorrow," a redheaded woman sang as the doors closed. "I've heard so many wonderful things about this speaker. Her presentation on leadership really helped Cliff put his business over the top. He found out he had been *managing*, not leading—and everything he thought he knew about leadership had been completely wrong."

"I just feel bad Morgan got sick and couldn't make it," a glamorous, blonde-haired woman with ample makeup and shiny bracelets sighed. "I still have her ticket—it's going to be wasted."

"Maybe we can find someone who needs it outside the theater. There are so many people looking to understand how to lead others with courage."

Hmn...a wasted ticket—for a presentation on leadership? I can't let that happen. I'm planning to hire people in the Fall. I don't want to screw up like that guy Cliff they were talking about.

But...what about Wheatie? What about my need to replenish my brain?

Dang it. I don't know a damn thing about leadership. I can't miss this opportunity.

"Um, excuse me," I intervened. "If you don't mind, may I ask the name of this speaker?"

My husband's eyes said it all: *Please don't do this. We are on vacation.*

I signaled him back in our own wordless form of communication: *Don't worry. It'll be fine...trust me.*

"Kym Glass," the redhead beamed, fishing through her leather briefcase.

Kym Glass—what a wonderful-sounding name.

"I think I have a flyer for her arena show in here somewhere."

"We came all the way from Virginia to see her," her blonde friend informed me. "True story—Kym escaped from a religious cult after thirty-five years. It's all in her book, *Unshakeable Courage.* I'm going to pick up a copy tomorrow and get it autographed."

She escaped from a cult? And wrote a book?

After having been involved in a business cult myself, I felt an immediate connection. It struck me as fate that I happened to be in this elevator with these two women. I *had* to hear Kym.

Wheatie desperately looked at where we were in terms of reaching our floor: We had another twenty to go.

"Here it is!" the redhead exclaimed, showing the flyer.

I looked at the colorful information sheet: a photo of an attractive woman about my age with long brown hair, grayish-blue eyes, and a warm smile. Above it appeared the following headlines:

Lead others with Courage to ***Fearless Freedom****!* *Understand and Apply the Seven Promises of* ***COURAGE***

This woman speaks my language!

The doors opened and the two ladies gathered their possessions to pass through them. "This is our floor," the blonde woman said to me. "Nice meeting you."

My hand involuntarily stretched out to hold the doors open. "Wait," I urged them. "I heard you say you had an extra ticket. How much is it? I mean…I'd like to attend, and I'll pay you for it."

Wheatie shrugged, helpless. I'm sure he thought this was inevitable. He'd seen me do this one too many times before.

"Are you a business owner?" flashed the redhead, once again scavenging in her briefcase.

"Yes," I replied. "I think I can learn a lot from Kym."

"Found it!" she announced, whipping out a ticket printout and presenting it to me. "It's yours. No charge."

Beaming from ear-to-ear, the two women stepped through the doors in order to avoid holding everyone up. My arm lowered to avoid blocking them. "No, I can't accept this!" I protested. The price listed on the piece of paper was far more than I could allow as a handout. "Really—I *insist*."

The blonde patted my hand: "It's on us. Don't worry about it. The ticket would probably have gone to waste, so consider it a gift. Enjoy!"

"Thank you, but—"

The doors closed before I had a chance to say anything further. I didn't even get their names.

I could feel Wheatie's eyes gazing at me, even though I continued to examine the ticket and flyer. "I can't take you anywhere—even on a vacation—without you doing some kind of work," he said.

"I'm so sorry," I said, holding him. "But you know how I am when I get an impulse like this. I just have to see it through.... It's only a few hours tomorrow morning. I promise—I'm all yours right afterward."

Wheatie nodded with approval. His mouth widened into a grin. "I guess I have no choice except to sleep in tomorrow and order in room service—lots of it!"

* * *

Kym Glass's event was much larger than I imagined: It was in an arena nearby that must have accommodated around 1,200 people. Every seat was occupied. I was so shocked and excited to discover that my free seat was located in the second row, center, right next to those two lovely ladies I had met in the elevator. How lucky was that—and in Vegas, too!

I became entranced by Kym the moment she took the stage in a designer black business suit with a pink blouse underneath. Draped around her neck was a lengthy white shawl with a gray pattern on it. Her jewelry—a silver necklace with oval patterns—was natural, but elegant. She radiated positive energy. When the applause died down, she addressed the crowd: "How many of you have ever seen someone at the top of the mountain—because they fell there?"

Oh my God...she's using my mountain metaphor. What are

139

the odds of that?!

"My first job was cold calling when I was fifteen years old. I worked in an office high school co-op call center. I sat around a boardroom table along with nine other people. Our manager came in and said, 'Welcome to your first day of work' and gave us all a large phonebook. Anyone remember what a phonebook is? I'm pretty sure I just gave you a flashback to another decade—probably another century."

Laughter ensued, including from Kym as she reflected back on that day.

"What I learned from this experience is that, by saying 'Yes' and having the courage, I could get to the top. I had to move quickly through countless phone rejections as I tried to sell tickets for special needs children to attend a local circus. The more calls I made, the better my chances were of finding those who would say, 'Yes!' By the time I left that company, I had learned valuable skills about cold calling and rejection. The most important part was not taking a 'no' response personally. These skills have continued to serve me through the years, as I have consistently reached out to others and built several connected communities.

"Another example of unshakeable courage that happened along my path: I was born fourth generation into a religious cult...."

Her voice slowed down for a pause as she seemed to swallow back her experiences. I admired the enormous courage it must have taken for her to overcome her fear. She had since made it to the other side, using her voice to inspire others to break free from the fears that had been preventing them from leading others with courage. The audience absorbed the information with a collective gasp.

"I made a difficult decision. I saw that the pattern of behavior that had happened among the three generations before me was about to be passed to my daughter. I could not sit by and allow my next generation to suffer. I knew that, if anything was going to change, it was for me to do something about it and take radical action to protect her."

On a screen behind Kym appeared a photo of a gorgeous blonde girl beside Kym as she continued: "Those of you who have children: How many of you would do more for your child than you would for yourself? You allowed yourself to go through things that you would not dare allow happen to your child. Momma bear would come charging out if anybody ever touched your kid. That is exactly where I was. I made a decision to break this toxic generational pattern and refused to allow what happened to me harm my child. I took a stand and mustered up courage from within myself. I didn't go to other cult member friends to share what happened to my family and me but, shortly after escaping, I planned a former member reunion with all of my forever friends in attendance. What I gained from this experience was worth more than twice what I thought I would lose—just by having the courage to say, 'I refuse to live in fear and allow this pattern to continue to my next generation.'

"I think back on everything that has happened to me along my journey. What if I hadn't said 'Yes' to learning about cold calling? Or if I hadn't said 'Yes' to escaping from that cult with my daughter? Or hadn't said 'Yes' to a twenty-plus year career in the telecom industry? Or said 'Yes' to a thriving entrepreneurial business and all of the various business opportunities that have come my way over the years? None of my success would have materialized. I didn't know the exact path. I didn't have it all figured out. I just said, 'Yes' to an opportunity, 'Yes' to a twenty-plus year corporate position, 'Yes' to a friend, and 'Yes' to a position. I have consistently and persistently let the path unfold.

"Today, I'm living in fearless freedom in every single area of my life. Whatever it is that you want to do, you have the courage within you to do it! Say 'Yes' to yourself and figure it out along the journey!"

Kym was not nearly finished, but the audience became overjoyed with her words and burst into applause. Teary-eyed, Kym accepted the warm response and continued on. She introduced her Seven Promises of Courage, supporting each phase of the roadmap she created through her experiences with concrete examples. Then she moved on to leadership.

"Influential leaders are those individuals who have the courage to *empower* other people, as opposed to *managing* them. They are in the trenches with their teams, nurturing them and helping them to achieve things they didn't think were possible. This doesn't mean they are doing things *for* their people or telling them exactly *how* to do things. They give them the tools and space to be able to figure it out on their own. Great leaders show their teams how they can take initiative and take a step back. Then, when the employees or teams need support, advice, or just a useful ear, those leaders are there for them and have their backs."

Influential leaders are those individuals who have the courage to empower *other people, as opposed to* managing *them. They are in the trenches with their teams, nurturing them and helping them to achieve things they didn't think were possible. This doesn't mean they are doing things* for *their people or telling them exactly* how *to do things. They give them the tools and space to be able to figure it out on their own.*
—Kym Glass

"It takes a great deal of courage and trust for leaders to empower their people. It also requires an enormous amount of honesty and transparency. These things are necessary in order to earn trust. If you are open with your teams, they will respect you and go the extra mile with you.

"Encourage *self*-leadership. This means that your team members are taking ownership for what they do: being open about what they don't know, asking questions, requesting help when they need it, and admitting when they make mistakes.

"One should never blame someone for his or her mistakes. I'm always curious when I hear someone on a team assign blame to someone else. Whether right or wrong, I wonder why that team member hasn't done what she could to help the other person through effective communication.

"We should be in the habit of championing ourselves—and each other because this is how we all win and be exceptional together!"

I soaked in everything Kym said while taking copious notes. I found myself drooling because all of her content was *soooo* good.

When she was done, the arena crowd greeted her with thunderous applause. She bowed, thanked us, and moved off the stage with a big wave and huge warm smile. I bolted out of my seat, determined to get a prime spot on her book signing line. I ended up being fourth. I purchased a copy of her book, *Unshakeable Courage*, and handed it to her for autographing. She grabbed a red Sharpie and opened up the cover to the title page. "Hi there," she smiled. "To whom would you like this written?"

"To Lynda Sunshine West," I said. "That's spelled 'Lynda' with a *y*—just like the 'y' in your name."

I knew I didn't have much time, as it felt like at least a hundred people were standing behind me, breathing down my neck. "I loved your presentation, Kym. I admit, I neglected my husband and my Vegas vacation to see you—and you totally made it worth my while."

"You did that for me?" she chuckled. "I'm honored anyone would do such a thing."

"Well, I'm a really driven entrepreneur, just like you. You totally spoke my language, especially with your mountain metaphor."

"I'm so glad, Lynda," she said, delicately writing a little note in the book.

"I just have a few questions for you, if you don't mind, as I'm going to be hiring and leading other people for the first time soon."

"Go ahead...you can ask while I'm personalizing your book."

"Do you think it's okay to be afraid of leading others? I mean, what if I'm not sure if I know the answer to something? Won't my people look to me to be right all of the time and have all of the answers?"

She paused in her writing to make full eye contact.

"What an excellent question, Lynda! You will *always* have some fear, but you can't let it hold you back. You must be courageous through fear with what I call 'fearless freedom' and instill your team with 'a daily dose of brave' to achieve the goal.

There will *always* be things along the way you simply don't know—or are unsure about. That's okay. Your team will appreciate seeing that you are human, just like them. But you still must act and make decisions. Your team will feel frustrated if you freeze up or take too long to get back to them. Never over-think a decision. I like to say, 'Stay out of the mental court. You have to get out of math class and launch!'"

---

*You must be courageous through fear with what
I call "fearless freedom" and instill your team
with "a daily dose of brave" to achieve the
goal. There will always be things along the way
you simply don't know—or are unsure about.
That's okay. Your team will appreciate seeing
that you are human, just like them. But you still
must act and make decisions. Your team will
feel frustrated if you freeze up or take too long
to get back to them. Never over-think a
decision. I like to say, "Stay out of the mental
court. You have to get out of math class and
launch!"*
—Kym Glass

"If you are ever in doubt about a request from an employee or team member—especially if it's something that might empower them—say, 'Yes' and then let them figure it out. You can't go wrong when you empower someone else. At the very least, if she makes a mistake, she will be learning something valuable by doing it on her own and will never repeat it."

"Got it," I said, scribbling down every single word.

She completed autographing the book. I thanked her profusely while clutching the book to my chest. "I'm going to start reading this right away while I'm lying by the pool later today."

"I never thought of it as poolside reading—but enjoy!" she laughed, handing me her business card. "Let's stay in touch, Lynda. I want to hear how everything turns out for you. Do you happen to have one for me?"

"Absolutely," I responded, exchanging my card for hers.

"Now go to your husband, thank him for sharing you with

us today, and have some fun!" she ordered.

"Yes. You're absolutely right," I agreed.

As soon as I stepped away from the crowd, I dialed Wheatie and made plans to meet him and reboot our vacation. I vowed to make it up to him—and to myself. It was time to have some fun.

Viva Las Vegas!

Bonus

Keeping the Momentum Going— Cutting Yourself (and Others) Some Slack

Pati Maez

Fall came and went. Thanks to the dozen people I had met along my mountainous journey, I accomplished everything I had set out to do. I conquered my mountain and crossed the finish line in fine fashion. My newly recruited employees proved to be eager pupils, and I could hardly contain myself from imparting all of my learnings on leadership to them on their very first day. (I resisted temptation and instead sprinkled in wisdom a little bit at a time…)

So, I wondered: What's next?

As I'd discovered over and over again, there is always some new lesson to be absorbed and some fresh insight to be gained each and every day. But I didn't anticipate that the source of my next gift—a bonus—had been hiding in plain sight all along: from my dear friend and colleague, Pati Maez.

Interestingly, Pati was the real deal when it came to mountain climbing. She was an avid weekend hiker who had checked off climbing many of the one hundred Southern California National Forest Peaks—including Mount Wilson and San Gorgonio Mountain—in preparation for a backpack trek in the Sierras to the top of Mount Whitney in California.

I greatly admired Pati in every respect—and not just her courage in braving mountain peaks. It seemed to me as if she had

147

done it all: former corporate executive (at Warner Bros. Pictures, no less!), entrepreneur, holistic life coach, spiritual teacher, motivational speaker, volunteer, award-winning artist, caregiver, playwright, author, and much more. She even sold real estate for a while. Pati is a true renaissance woman.

I loved hearing her tell the story of how, at the age of six, after witnessing the bruising of domestic violence, she stomped her right foot and declared, "From now on, I am a businesswoman!" Imagine being so perceptive at such a young age; at the time she had thought that proving yourself as a strong, successful woman was one potential way for women to avoid such abuse.

She certainly went on to become a businesswoman—a successful entrepreneur—and a whole lot more, founding UNIV OF SOUL, a resource center serving those who are open to expanding and expounding on their innate gifts and talents to serve others. As an example, Pati developed The Maez Method, a breathing technique that I utilize on a regular basis and is part of her system called The 7-Spiritual Essentials for Business Success. These *essentials* guide women in transition to enhance relationships and build a business with exponential growth. If that's not enough, Coach Pati works tirelessly to stop domestic violence and abuse. She strives to comfort at least one client a day to ease her struggles and suffering.

Over the years, Pati had become what I refer to as my "Spiritual Mama." I'd heard others describe her as "the Candid Coach." She's somewhat of an ethereal spiritual person with an open and generous heart. She is a truly kind and compassionate person, but also no-nonsense when it comes to business and playful and funny when engaging with friends and clients.

I admit I hesitated at first when Pati asked me to travel with her to Sedona, Arizona, and join her on a hike—especially since she referenced going to a place called Devil's Bridge.

Devil's Bridge! There is NO WAY I am going to brave any kind of real mountain—not with a name like that!

"You've got to be kidding me, Pati! I can barely go up a department store escalator without getting dizzy."

"Don't be silly, Lynda," she dismissed. "It's not anything like it sounds. It's just a hike, not a major climb. It's one of the easiest trails and the hike is pretty short. Sure, there are a few steps to go up, but trust me, you'll gain so many benefits from it. It's a mystical experience with breathtaking views. Come on, have I ever led you astray?"

"No...I guess not," I conceded, though with some remaining trepidation.

Eventually, I caved in and agreed to join her. Pati is an influencer of many different things. In hindsight, I should have known that she had an underlying purpose for luring me out to Devil's Bridge; as I would later discover, it had nothing whatsoever to do with addressing my fear of heights or my ability to climb a mountain.

* * *

Pati was right that the Devil's Bridge Trail was easy to get to and wasn't overly daunting. The entire hike was only a couple of miles each way. I watched little kids traversing the path and figured: *If they can do it, so can I.*

The weather was spectacular: mid-70s, sunny, and not a cloud in the sky. The mountain ahead was postcard-worthy and unlike anything I'd ever seen. As we stepped forward, I couldn't take my eyes off the red-tinted soil beneath our feet. I was surprised to find that there was almost as much greenery—including cacti and yucca—as there were rocks along the path. We climbed up and down various small hills, which caused my heart to pulse a bit from scrambling on the rocks. I admit that Pati had to lend her hand to me more than once and give me constant reassurance that I was doing great and would be safe.

149

We reached the top of Devil's Bridge. The view of the landscape was so beautiful it made me forget to feel petrified. It more than lived up to Pati's billing as "mystical."

We found the perfect spot by a shady tree to sit down for a rest. A moment later, as I guzzled some water, Pati pulled out her animal cards and asked if I wanted a reading. She knew that I would enjoy whatever insights she might offer to me.

"Yes, I'd love an animal card," I excitedly answered.

"Lynda," she stated, gently placing down an animal card, "Here we go. Are you ready?"

"You bet!"

"Let's see...wow! What do you know! Look at this, Lynda—the Jaguar appeared. The Jaguar is all about being honest with yourself, holding yourself accountable, and taking responsibility for speaking impeccably. The animal represents telling the truth from your core essence. This takes immense practice, especially when old patterns of blame, shame, and guilt show up—even if you have done a ton of self-development work. Putting it bluntly: Judgment and doubt creeps in when you least expect it, and what others say or think of you shows up and throws you off balance.

"To quote Eleanor Roosevelt: 'What other people think of me is none of my business.' This concept has kept me honest and focused on what matters most: living on purpose, both personally and professionally. Practicing this perspective of integrity and impeccability has been a lifesaver in many different situations throughout my life.

"Lynda, do you recall when you asked me: 'Do you remember the first time you lied?' My answer was 'yes'; it was a life-changing experience for me. That little white lie led to another and another, until I broke down and admitted that I had lied—to my mother, no less. That experience almost killed me. I felt so much shame and guilt for trying to hide and cover up what I had said and done.

"I discovered that I was more concerned with how my mother viewed me than I was about telling the whole truth. I came to realize that I wasn't perfect, and I needed to cut myself some slack. More importantly, I had to forgive myself. I didn't need to hide or pretend to be something I wasn't. All I needed to do was hold myself accountable and take one hundred percent responsibility for my actions. Since then, this has positively impacted most areas of my life.

"I love that Jaguar showed up for you today. This may be some of the best medicine any of us can swallow," Pati reflected. "I've always been candid with you, right Lynda?"

Uh-oh. The other shoe is about to drop. Yeah, but it's another perspective from Pati, so it should be okay.

"Yup, you've always been direct with me," I gulped. "All right, tell me: What have I done wrong?"

"Nothing, Lynda—you haven't done anything wrong at all. You know I don't come from a place of right or wrong. What would make you think that?" she waved. "To some extent, I'm suggesting that you have a choice of embracing a different perspective from this day forward, if you choose this new path. Information I've gathered and observed from you and my intuition have led me to the perspective I am about to offer you."

What could she possibly mean?

"Do you recall my coining the expression 'I didn't know to know'?"

"Yes," I answered, wondering where she was going with this.

"You've asked a dozen or so people for advice and wisdom and have benefited from all of these wonderful people. There is one area—one blind spot—you didn't know to ask about. It's the one missing *essential* you must have in order for your momentum to continue into your next journey," she said. "Actually, it's the *first essential* to business success. When I said 'journey,' I'm referring to Arthur Ashe's quote: 'Success is a journey, not a destination.' In other words, you don't have to be so concerned with the end result when you have a plan and a strategy for an intentional goal you want to manifest. You must be committed to the journey.

"Some people hide behind the *doing* and avoid facing their fears by performing distracting activities. They are like children wearing suits of armor. They put on hard outer shells, which hide their soft developing bodies. Some people do one thing and barely complete it before moving on to the next without making time to rejuvenate or refuel. They rush to the next activity without reflecting and absorbing lessons learned. Some live for the next thing without being in the moment."

I drew a total blank.

What is she talking about?

"You look worried and befuddled, Lynda," she chuckled. "You don't need to be either. Just relax and I'll explain everything to you. I'll save the most important point—the blind spot—for last."

"Okay, hit me with it. I can take it. I'm ready," I stated, steeling myself for the worst.

What could be so important to tell me that we had to travel seven hours to get here and then labor on this hike?

"I'll give it to you straight, just like I always do. My first impression of you was that you were a woman struggling to come out from a dark place, as if you were hiding your truth. I felt as if negative emotional energies were controlling your attitude. It inadvertently manifested itself as being rude, abrupt, and intrusive. The first time we met, you interrupted a conversation I was having. You made a judgmental statement that I was being 'too salesy' when all I was doing was answering a question. But then I instantly remembered that earlier you'd introduced yourself to the group as 'I'm Lynda Sunshine West, and I'm in transition.' I admired and appreciated that. I paused and then leaned into you, as if looking into my own reflection. I recognized an energy, a deep-seated anxiety and a wounded sadness. At the same time, there was also loving compassion coming through your heart space. I felt a woman who was desperate and yearning for more—something of a diamond in the rough.

"You have come such a long way since then, my sister! You are so generous sharing your skills and always so eager to help others to succeed. You are determined to get what you want. You work so hard to 'get shit done'—'finishit fast,' as you say. You are constantly trying to learn and improve yourself. All of these are magnificent qualities...."

"I hear a 'but' coming on," I inserted.

"No 'but,'" she smiled. "You know I believe the word 'but' would negate everything I said before. What I said then continues to apply and I have something else: You are still in transition."

"I *am*? But I've gained so much momentum—I can feel that I've achieved a great deal of success," I defended myself.

"All true," Pati concurred. "You have taken great strides. I also know that sometimes you either rush to get things done or quit on them before you get to the finish line, as if you know you are going to lose—or that it won't manifest to what you set out for. I've noticed—and from what I've heard you share with me—that you make thousands of calls for other entrepreneurs...but you don't do it for yourself. It's as if sometimes you do things just to check them off and say they are done when they are only half-baked.

"Sometimes I wonder if you avoid completing a task because you're afraid of being judged by the final result. In other words, you find it easier to portray yourself as having

153

dropped out, rather than having failed."

She has me pegged. She sees right through me.

"Also, you aren't always transparent with me. You know I expect honesty from all of my friends and clients—especially my sisters in business."

I lowered my head, knowing exactly what she was talking about. Recently, I had put myself in an awkward position by not telling her the whole truth about something. I should have expected she would figure it out. She's too sharp and intuitive to have the wool pulled over her eyes. At the time I immediately said, "you're right," fessed up, and apologized.

Pati had previously taught me that: "Conscious omissions—or telling so-called little white lies—have consequences. They can be old habits that require vigilance in order to prevent them from creeping back."

These are great lessons for me to remember. Although she forgave me and didn't hold a grudge, this clearly remained an area of personal improvement for me.

I realized the perspective she was sharing. Like what Pati had done with her mother, I had omitted telling her the whole truth because I was more concerned with how she would view me than I was with complete honesty. I grasped what she had said earlier: If I were to cut myself some slack it would eliminate the self-imposed pressure to look good and allow me an easier space to be more authentic.

"I got it!" I exclaimed.

"That's great, Lynda!" she stated. "I'd like to acknowledge you for that new awareness. We definitely need to embrace vigilance to not allow the old habits and patterns to control our very essence. And, if they do creep in, which they may, make sure to cut yourself some slack, and focus on being your current and future best self. We must accept the fact that we are works in progress, not perfect beings. You have a huge heart and you're brilliant, Lynda—a quick study, for sure."

"I have a feeling there's more...."

"Just one more thing," she said.

Dang, why did I agree to this climb? Hearing all of this frank, constructive feedback is way scarier than any part of this mountain climb.

"I love you, Lynda, you know that. I have always supported you, and will continue to have your back," she assured me.

I nodded, feeling tears well up.

"I also encourage you to be aware that you sometimes have a lot of noise going on in your head. There are times when I don't feel your head and heart are engaged; it's like your body is communicating one thing and your words are saying something else."

"What do you mean? I'm not disagreeing...I'm just trying to understand."

"I'm talking about getting conscious, clear, and congruent by engaging your head and your heart to unlock your core essence: your intuition. How about we ask the animals again? I know you enjoy getting insight from the cards. That will help me explain this last part," she said.

I nodded affirmatively.

"Okay, Lynda. Here's the last card. Awesome—it's Dolphin medicine," she squealed with delight. "I got goosebumps. The Dolphin is exactly what I wanted to share with you on this trip. This medicine is all about your spiritual power and stepping into your intuitive knowing—yet remaining humble for the greater good of everyone. I know you have already stepped into your courage by 'facing a fear a day.' You even wrote a book about it entitled *The Year of Fears*.

"Because of that, you now know and understand the things that scare you the most. These are lessons you can share with your eager pupils.

"Lynda, the ultimate purpose of this hike was for us to be out in the wilderness experiencing the pure essence of Dolphin medicine, the *mana* of life—the *breath* of being one with nature, aligned with the universe, and honest from the core. Let's pause for a moment and look out at the vista. Take a deep breath, if that feels right to you. Feel the cool breeze on your lovely skin, and the warmth from the sun shining on your beautiful cheeks."

I followed her instructions.

"Lynda, what do you see out there? You don't have to answer right now. I'm only asking you to acknowledge how the external realm impacts the internal self. What are the feelings and thoughts that are flooding your mind, your heart, or both? Take this moment to notice how your body is feeling and what it speaks."

We paused to feel the air and take note of the peaks and valleys and the Red Rock formations. The moment felt especially good.

"Lynda, when we get back to San Diego, I invite you to make more time for stillness and quiet. It is critical that you silence your busy mind and get clear with who you are. Discover what you truly love and are passionate about in order to receive what you want moving forward. I've found that the most successful people in business make time to still their minds. They leave room for fresh ideas before embarking on the next journey.

"The most important thing to do is to breathe and CAG— center, align, and ground—into yourself. When we get back, I can share more with you. Then I will guide you to embrace quiet, which will enable you to become conscious, clear, and congruent. This will allow you to innovate and collaborate for the greater good of all."

"Is there something specific I can learn now?"

Pati clapped her hands together with joy: "Ha! You're always so eager to jump right in and get things done, Lynda! I love that about you. All action all the time. Again, you're all about: 'Finishit fast!' Perhaps you can make time to review your business plan and strategy and then take the necessary steps based on what you have intentionally set out to do. Become clear with what you wish to manifest as you move forward. You need to get specific, right down to the details.

"You might also want to consider what you can do outside of your business and your immediate network. Perhaps you can give back to your community and serve them, too. There is nothing more noble and rewarding than volunteering and devoting your time to serving others—especially if you don't receive money or some other business payback for your work. I congratulate you on how much you've done in the past, and maybe it is time to step up your game even further."

There is nothing more noble and rewarding than volunteering and devoting your time to serving others—especially if you don't receive money or some other business payback for your work. I congratulate you on how much you've done in the past, and maybe it is time to step up your game even further.
—Pati Maez

"I do have one idea on how to make that happen," I offered.

"Excellent—I'd love to hear it!" Pati said.

"I've been thinking about expanding my nonprofit, The Giving Angels. I welcome your counsel on how to handle it."

"I love the idea!" Pati roared with approval. "Let's set a time to help you make that happen when we get back. I'd be pleased to share my wisdom and knowledge to have you accomplish this new path."

"Deal!" I exclaimed. "Thank you so much for all of your help, Pati. I don't know what I'd do without you. You're so honest and direct with me. You help me address the emotional side of life. I can always count on you for telling it like it is—even if it's tough medicine for me to swallow. I really appreciate it."

"That's what sisters are for—to provide different perspectives and to hold up a mirror," she said, hugging me.

Sisters—I like the sound of that.

"So...what do you think is next for me?"

"Oh, my goodness! Lynda, Lynda, Lynda: stop!" Pati laughed. "You're doing it again. Stop to get still and quiet...to breathe and CAG—center, align, and ground into mama earth. Allow your spirit, your God, your intuition to guide you.

"This is the first and most important *essential* to accomplish in life. Florence Scovel-Shinn, my favorite mentor, describes this beautifully in her book, *The Game of Life and How to Play It*: 'Whatsoever a man soweth, that shall he also reap.' In other words, everything you think, say, do, eat, and drink determines what you will attract and eliminate from your life. The message is clear: You must make time to pause, breathe, and be specific with what you wish to manifest.

"Let's take a moment. Close your eyes. Breathe in the fresh air, release all of the noise in the out breath, and relax into your body. Stop all of the chatter and take in all of this beauty. There's nothing to do—only *to be*. Allow yourself to be in this moment. You're on such an amazing journey, and it is time to relish the moment. You can count on the fact that there will always be the next thing. The most important things for you to consider: take responsibility, hold yourself accountable, and be impeccable when confronted or triggered by old negative emotions that creep up unexpectedly. When you don't, you must cut yourself some slack.

"Be like Jaguar: honest with yourself, no matter how scary it may seem or feel. This will take practice. The more you do it, the more you'll notice the magnificent ripple impacting many others from your new perspective.

"Let's now enjoy this glorious moment. As soon as we climb down, we are going to celebrate!" Pati declared.

"Celebrate? Celebrate what?" I asked.

"The next mountain you are about to climb, of course! Better yet, let's start celebrating on the way back to the trailhead. Remember: It's not the destination, it's the journey to success in serving others. Some journeys have no end."

Pati linked arms with me, started down the trail, and called out, "Come on, Lynda, let's go!"

MOMENTUM

Contributor Biographies

*The contributors would love to hear from you! For a link to
their websites to contact them, go to:*
www.MomentumTheBook.com

David (Dave) Blackford is founder of Blacklock Designs, an umbrella name and hub for his various products. There is one special item he sells that is not one of his inventions: A-Leg-Up®. His father designed it to provide a stable and comfortable platform to perform tasks such as pedicures, trimming nails, putting on socks and shoes, and spraying foot powder or lotion. If you would like to view this product, go to www.a-leg-up.com.

Amy Burton is a thriving business owner with a diverse entrepreneurial background. Her million dollar company, Revel Salon and Color Studio, is located in Lake Wylie, South Carolina. She is an author, a Certified Canfield Success Principles Trainer/Speaker/ Coach, a RIM® Facilitator and is an UNBLINDED™ Sales Mastery Coach. Amy is a board member of Rise Together International, Inc., a nonprofit organization bringing hope and healing to impoverished families.

Annie Evans is a Best-Selling Author, coach, speaker—helping people to become their best selves. Her life experience has empowered her to help others conquer fear and uncertainty to meet life's challenges. A jack-of-many-trades, she took a start-up from $7mil to $25mil. She is a Start-Over Expert—more at LiveForANewDay.com. CA Realtor®, DRE# 00702725.

Nadia Fleury is an entrepreneur, executive alchemist coach, and founder and CEO of Avesence® skin care products. She is also creator of Infinite Mastermind Alliance™, which features her specialized programs designed to help clients connect their vision into a custom strategy that mixes mindset, wisdom, and business knowledge to find success.

Kym Glass is a soft skills consultant, award-winning speaker, and bestselling author with more than twenty years of corporate experience and eighteen years as a business owner. She is author of the book *Unshakeable Courage*.

Don Green (Foreword) is CEO and executive director of The Napoleon Hill Foundation. He is author of *Everything I Know about Success I Learned from Napoleon Hill*.

Dennis Haber is an author, speaker, and Ziglar Legacy Certified Trainer and Coach, as well as a DISC Certified Behavior Consultant. His book, *Don't Play With Fire: How To Keep Your Greatness From Going Up In Flames*, helps people live as if they are living a second time—but this time wiser and smarter.

Sohaila Handelsman is a world-renowned belly dancing millionaire entrepreneur expert. She is also an artist, dance instructor, and sought-after choreographer. She is the founder of Sohaila International, an umbrella of her various programs, including NewVo® Fitness and her signature Sense-ual Woman™ retreats and courses. She is author of four books and a set of course workbooks; the creator of a dozen dance signature instruction videos; and producer of over 400 online videos. She empowers female entrepreneurs to gain clarity, shimmy into their superpowers, and gain unshakeable Confidence to attract their ideal clients.

Ron Klein (Wise Man), who has been dubbed the "Grandfather of Possibilities," is best known as the inventor of the credit card magnet strip. He is also the creator of the credit card validity checking system and the developer of computerized systems for real estate Multiple Listing Services (MLS), voice response for the banking industry, and bond quotation and trade information for the New York Stock Exchange. Ron is the founder and CEO of Technitrend, Inc. and General Associates, Inc.

Pati Maez is the founder and CEO of UNIV OF SOUL, a resource center that specializes in spiritual experiences combining East/West philosophies with intuitive natural wisdom. For the co-active participants, this offers the opportunity for personal and business transformational growth. She has dedicated her life to creating and teaching The Maez Method, a breathing technique utilized with The 7-Spiritual Essentials for Business Success. Pati, who worked as an

163

executive at Warner Bros. Motion Pictures, is currently a successful entrepreneur, holistic life coach, spiritual guide, award-winning artist, playwright, author, and social media influencer.

Krysten Maracle invested 35 years as a civilian at Naval Information Warfare Center Pacific in San Diego, California, with Joint Services (Navy, Army, Air Force and Marines) in various roles: Computer Scientist, Program Manager, Contracting Officer Representative and retired December 2019. She is a philanthropist, Executive Producer of WishMan Movie, founding member of the Mastermind Association, and Founder of Maracle Mastermind, conducting interviews, supporting others, solving challenges and exploring new opportunities. Her travels include Amsterdam, Australia, Austria, Bahamas, Belgium, Bulgaria, Canada, China, Croatia, Czech Republic, France, Germany, Greece, Hungary, India, Ireland, Italy, Malaysia, Mexico, Netherlands, Singapore, Turkey, United Arab Emirates (UAE), and United Kingdom.

Elizabeth Moors is the founder of Taking Charge of You, which provides online and seminar training in personal development and Aspergers. Her book. *Taking Charge of You*, was a bestseller and a finalist in the International Book Awards.

Michael (Mike) Packman is the founder of Keystone National Properties. Packman began his career more than twenty-five years ago in the finance industry. In 2003, Packman formed his own diversified financial company which he successfully exited. After the downturn in 2008, he became involved in the real estate space, initially focusing heavily on 1031 exchanges. He is also the cofounder of Bundlefi, a financial technology start-up where he serves as Vice-Chairman and COO. Packman speaks at large and small events, including nationally recognized family office and other business conferences. He has shared the stage with world-renowned business leaders, including Tony Robbins. Packman is the 1031 expert contributor for the *New York Real Estate Journal* and has been featured in the *Real Deal.*

Paige Panzarello, the "Cashflow Chick," is the founder of The Tryllion Group and an investor/entrepreneur, having done $150 Million+ in real estate transactions. She currently specializes in Non-Performing Notes. She has been a regularly featured guest on "The Cashflow Guys" podcast, the "Best Ever Show" with Joe Fairless, and many other real estate and entrepreneurial podcasts, as well as in *The Wall Street Journal.* She also speaks at various different real estate investing clubs and conferences across the country. Paige teaches the "Building Wealth with Notes" workshop that drills down into the details of how to successfully buy Non-Performing Notes, create passive income, and mitigate risk.

Dr. Greg Reid (Wise Man), who received his honorary PhD in literature, is considered one of the top five keynote speakers by *Forbes* and *Entrepreneur.* He has been published in more than seventy books, which have been translated into forty-five languages. Among his bestselling books are *Stickability, Three Feet from Gold,* and *Wealth Made Easy.*

Frank Shankwitz (Wise Man), best known as co-founder of the Make-A-Wish® Foundation, has received the President's Call to Service, the Making a Difference in the World, the Making a World of Difference, and the Ellis Island Medal of Honor awards. He is author of the autobiographical book *Wish Man*, which was adapted to film in 2019.

Brian Smith (Wise Man), the founder of UGG Boots, is an innovator, keynote speaker, and author of *Birth of a Brand*.

Lynda Sunshine West, creator of Women Action Takers, is a philanthropist, speaker, and author. She is founder and president of The Giving Angels—a 501(c)(3) nonprofit whose mission is to eradicate homelessness once and for all. The bestselling author of *The Year of Fears*, Lynda resides in Alpine, California.

CPSIA information can be obtained
at www.ICGtesting.com
Printed in the USA
BVHW030253100123
655931BV00001B/4